Wellness, Spirituality and Sports

THOMAS RYAN

Paulist Press
New York/Mahwah

The Publisher gratefully acknowledges the use of excerpts from *Fit or Fat* by Covert Bailey. Copyright © 1977, 1978 by Covert Bailey. Reprinted by permission of Houghton Mifflin Company.

A chart from p. 226 of *Total Swimming* by Harvey S. Wiener, copyright © 1980 by Harvey S. Wiener is reprinted by permission of Simon & Schuster, Inc.

Library of Congress Cataloging-in-Publication Data

Ryan, Thomas, Father.
    Wellness, spirituality, and sports.

    Bibliography: p.
    1. Exercise—Religious aspects—Christianity.
2. Sports—Religious aspects—Christianity. I. Title
RA781.R93   1986   248.4   86-4923
ISBN 0-8091-2801-2 (pbk.)

Published by Paulist Press
997 Macarthur Boulevard
Mahwah, New Jersey 07430

Printed and bound in the
United States of America

Contents

Acknowledgements

to the staff members of the Canadian Centre for Ecumenism for their various enabling roles, encouragement and interest;

to Suzanne Gagnon, Mary Mooney and Marianne Cooper for their valuable assistance in proofreading;

to Bernard Campbell, C.S.P. for his editorial direction and assistance.

Sincere thanks.

Dedicated to
all my "coaches"
in the sporting and spiritual realms
who never lost sight
of the points of connection
between the two:

James Korth
Ron Wright
Arling Anderson
Jack Campbell, SJ
Joseph Occhio, SDB
Peter Granzotto, SDB
Harry Rasmussen, SDB
Marian Cross
John McGinn, CSP
George Fitzgerald, CSP
Ria Waters
John Main, OSB

But yield who will to their separation,
My object in living is to unite
My avocation and my vocation
As my two eyes make one in sight.
Only where love and need are one,
And the work is play for mortal stakes,
Is the deed ever really done
For Heaven and the future's sakes.

"Two Tramps In Mud Time"

Robert Frost

Chapter 1

The Wellness Revolution

Choose life—only that and always
and at whatever risk.
Christ came that we might have life
and have it more abundantly.
The world is full of false prophets
who will tell you otherwise.
To let life leak out, to let it wear away
by the mere passage of time,
to withhold giving it and spending it,
is to choose nothing.
The ultimate betrayal
of your faith and your education
is not to choose life
with all of the anguish and terror and delight
which are attendant upon that choice.

Helen Kelley

The fitness craze and the search for spiritual meaning are two of the greatest hungers in North American life today. The numbers of people making their way to retreat houses or Bible study groups, sessions on centering prayer or Ignatian meditation, desert days or spirituality courses are only to be exceeded by the jump in membership at Nautilus training centers, YM or YWCA's, aerobic clubs and a host of other new multipurpose health club facilities. But little energy has been expended in trying to assist the millions who are involved in the pursuit of one or the other to connect the two.

The question could be framed in various ways, but a letter from my sister-in-law (with whom I have at various times canoe-camped, skied, played racquetball, swum, and jogged) sets it forth with admirable clarity:

> There is something that has always been hard for me to understand. I can fit in running with my responsibilities as a mother of a 2 and a 4 year old; work for my husband as a surgical assistant, secretary, gopher, and janitor; maintain our household and be involved in a few community activities. But when I try to incorporate a little spirituality via reading or prayer, my good intentions last only for a night or two.
>
> I can finagle an hour to run or an hour to ski in preparation for a race, but not talk to my kids about God. I will not eat all day prior to a long run late in the afternoon, but I can't maintain an abstinence on Ash Wednesday or Good Friday. I can put up with sub-zero temperatures, blisters, and sore

muscles, but can't follow through on Lenten goals. And yet my sporting activities have provided some of the most inspirational times of my life and the acknowledgement that, yes, there is truly a God.

I remember in particular one day skiing at French Rapids. It was snowing and I had been skiing for some time. The trees were laden with snow, the track was filled in and all I could hear were my skis going through the snow. So quiet and so beautiful. Great inspiration for then—but not later that night, or the next day in church.

It seems that the human qualities underlying sporting activity are the same for spirituality, but I haven't made the transition. I can make myself run as hard as I can for 10 kilometers with my lungs screaming and legs aching, or herringbone up one last hill on cross-country skis and then kick and glide as hard as I can the last kilometer of the race, but I can't make myself listen to the entire homily or ponder a short daily reading.

I've reached a new level this winter in cross-country skiing and am aiming for one in running the marathon next summer. My efforts in these regards have brought me to a new level of fitness and developed different abilities, as well as resulting in an improved self-concept. But what about my spiritual life? And now, of course, my children are pressing the issue. The struggle continues. . . .

This book is one person's answer to her question. It is written in the conviction that those who share the question and the struggle are legion. As one involved in athletic and church activities all my life, I have lived and wrestled with that question very personally, in the spirit of Rainer Maria Rilke's poem:

Be patient toward all that is unsolved
in your heart,

and try to love the questions themselves. . . .
And the point is to live everything,
to live the questions now.
Perhaps you will gradually,
without noticing it,
live along some distant day
into the answer.

   The integration of themes contained in these pages represents my "living the question out into an answer."

   The context for the discussion is Wellness. Born in the tofu-and-sandals culture of the 1970's, it is a holistic approach to health whose time has finally come. The signs of its serious acceptance have been many. To cite but one: toward the end of 1984, when the United Auto Workers signed what amounted to a revolutionary contract with General Motors stressing job security over pay increases, one innovative clause provided for "wellness benefits." The acknowledgement of the concept in a major labor agreement marks a milestone of sorts: the pursuit of wellness has now joined the roster of inalienable American rights. Even corporations have finally begun to recognize that the great ideal of *mens sana in corpore sano* makes a great deal of sense.

   In the way of such trends, the wellness vogue is becoming a thriving industry in itself. An army of energy and fitness trainers-stress managers has sprung up, bringing their services not only to business concerns but to such diverse consumers as the Los Angeles Fire Department and the Girl Scouts of America. Yet, according to T. George Harris, editor of *American Health* magazine, "The idea is still so new that no single corporate executive knows how to put it all together yet. There is no adequate theory of it."

   To my mind, one of the reasons why existing theories to date have been inadequate is that they have neglected an essential human component: spirituality. The abundance of life sought in the various wellness programs is both our human and our spiritual aim. In pursuing the conditions for and seeking to experience for ourselves the quality of abundant life, we are engaged on an eminently spiritual quest. No life-promising doctrine and no salvation can perform something we have not already undertaken for ourselves.

That is why the holistic health vision of wellness is the best framework available for responding to the question posed by my sister-in-law. She is quite right; the human qualities underlying sporting activities are the same as those underlying spiritual life activities. Discipline, dedication, enthusiasm, and perseverance are a few of the human qualities. The "raw material," if you will, is the same; the difference is in the application. Millions of people have the raw material and only apply it in one direction, i.e., sports, when the same basic human virtues at work there could also be bringing them rich spiritual experience.

There are two "wires" there which have the potential to carry a high voltage current; they only need to be connected. The "connector" is a holistic vision of health and vitality seen in terms of *all* the dimensions of the human person.

Wellness as the Context for the Discussion

Up until now, our approach to health has been largely negative. We have focused on how to repair injuries or cure disease. What we are witnessing in the wellness revolution is a further development of the growing consciousness about holistic health care. Professionals in the field are calling this positive, holistic approach *wellness*. The basic idea is to enhance the quality of our lives by making health not just the absence of disease but the presence of a high-level energy and a sense of well-being. The keys that open the door to wellness are generally identified as personal responsibility, nutrition, physical fitness, stress management, and a sensitivity to one's environment. The conviction is that well-being is less mystical than we have been led to believe, and has a great deal to do with empirical and practical measures within the range of everyone.

The idea that grace builds on nature or that grace perfects nature has long been a truism of the spiritual life. Inasmuch as wellness programs seek to integrate harmoniously all the various components of a person's life, theologians should rejoice. A new cultural movement is helping them recover and set forth clearly the ancient Hebraic idea of the indivisible unity of the human person which lies at the heart of the Hebrew Scriptures or Old Testament.

One of these theologians is John J. Pilch, a biblical scholar who, while lecturing and writing extensively on Scripture, health and wellness, is also professor of preventive medicine at the Medical College of Wisconsin. In his book, *Wellness: Your Invitation to Full Life* (Winston Press, 1981), he identifies five key elements in the concept of wellness:

- Knowing the purpose and meaning of life;
- Identifying life's authentic, satisfying, fulfilling human joys and pleasures;
- Accepting responsibility for freedom of self-determination in life;
- Finding an appropriate source of motivation (spiritual values and/or religious beliefs);
- Accepting the need for change in life, the need for ongoing "conversion."

As these five elements indicate, wellness is a lifestyle, a way of living. "You could be terminally ill, mentally retarded, permanently disabled . . . and still have a high level of wellness," writes Pilch. "Or, conversely, you could be a glowing picture of physical and mental health but not have the foggiest notion of a direction in life, and therefore have a very low level or no level of wellness." Spiritual values and religious beliefs play a legitimate and important role in the pursuit of wellness.

A wellness orientation contrasts with the way most of us have long thought about our health. We typically consider ourselves physically well if we do not need the services of a doctor or if we don't have to take medications too regularly, or if we have no major discomforts. We consider ourselves spiritually healthy if we go to church fairly regularly, engage in an acceptable amount of devotions, and stay away from obvious, major sins. We often consider ourselves emotionally healthy if we can avoid "feeling lousy" much of the time or do not have to visit a counselor, psychologist, or psychiatrist. Health, by these definitions, is merely the absence of illness. It involves only a minimum level of functioning.

A wellness orientation is more positive. People seeking *physical* wellness enjoy many benefits. They put their bodies through strenuous exercise and choose not to eat what many of us find to be irresistibly appealing because they have discovered that their lives are better now with regular exercise and right-eating than they were before. Their hearts are more efficient. They have more energy, and they have less of a chance of suffering from diseases linked to contemporary eating habits. Higher levels of physical health may lead to a corresponding increase in productivity for their work, their families, and their church.

People seeking *spiritual* wellness identify a new sense of commitment and satisfaction in their worship, work, and play. They experience a fuller spiritual life than those of us who are satisfied with the minimum daily requirements. Their close communion with God and their extensive sharing with fellow-believers in praise and service lead to profound changes throughout their lives.

People seeking *emotional* wellness often find more enjoyment in themselves and their relationships. Many become more productive in their work. They learn to manage stress in conflict. They communicate in ways that allow for better understanding and mutual acceptance. They rebuild relationships for responsibility and mutual benefit. For many there are profound changes in their inner lives and their relationships.

Wellness enables us to move toward that full humanness which represents God's dream for us: "The glory of God is the human person fully alive." In seeking wellness we no longer are content with the minimum but seek to *maximize* our use of God's gifts. Correspondingly, our homage to God is greater when we function with increased physical, spiritual, and emotional vitality.

Yet, the orientation of wellness programs has to be approached discerningly. As Dr. John Travis, M.D., stresses in "What Is Meant by Wellness" (*Holistic Health Handbook,* by the Berkeley Holistic Health Center, And/Or Press, Berkeley, 1978, p. 97), overemphasis on one approach is to be avoided. Too many advisers, he feels, think the way to well-being lies only in their special area. For example, nutrition enthusiasts too often ignore stress control; some stress-control teachers dismiss physical awareness; and some physical fitness buffs give no place to the spirit. If there is one principle about which Travis is adamant, it is the value of integrating the different dimensions into a *balanced* approach to well-being.

But, insists Pilch, wellness is more than just a superior condition of health. In fact, it is conceivable that wellness would not necessarily lead to what would be considered, for example, good physical health. "You can be an Olympic gold-medal winner capturing every medal in your specialty but be unable to get along with any fellow Olympians," attests Pilch. "In other words, you can be the epitome of health but not have any level of wellness. You can come out of your physician's office 'fit as a fiddle' or 'healthy as a horse' but then go home and beat your spouse or abuse your children with all your health and strength. Healthy? Unquestionably. Well? Not at all!"

Wellness can coexist with chronic illness, disease and even terminal illness, since it extends to and includes non-physical aspects of life. Further, whereas there is a definite point at which one passes from health to sickness or vice versa, wellness is a never-ending process, an ever-expanding experience. Even while possessing wellness, one pursues higher levels of it.

Wellness: A Holistic Approach to Health Care

We have much to recover from the lessons of the past. The explosion of material technology has cluttered our inner and outer world, covering over the simple natural laws of the universe. Wellness is particularly relevant for this time as it calls us to value and trust ourselves, making harmoniously one the inner and the outer, thinking and feeling.

The writings of the Greek teacher Hippocrates indicate he clearly grasped that medicine, science, and philosophy were not separate disciplines, but one great discourse on life. Our twentieth-century beliefs, conceived largely in the eighteenth-century Age of Reason, have dichotomized body and mind and virtually exiled spirit altogether. The wellness revolution signals a rebirth of our appreciation for integral wholeness, unity, and flow.

The word "health" is itself formed from the Anglo-Saxon *hai,* meaning *whole,* and is defined as a "flourishing condition of well-being, vitality, prosperity." It implies that all aspects of the total system are in balance with one another, that physical, emotional, mental, and spiritual needs are being met in the proper proportion. If the needs of each aspect of being are satisfied, then each will be properly tuned to the others, like instruments in an orchestra. Each person is a delicately balanced spiritual-psychophysical system. If one section of the orchestra is out of tune, then the harmony of the whole is disturbed. As an example of the more holistic approach of some currents in contemporary medicine, Dick Anderson, an educational planner for the University of California, speaks in terms of physical poisons that can disturb the physical system, and mental, emotional, and spiritual poisons that can disturb the subjective system. These "subjective poisons" include such things as uncaring thoughts, feelings, and actions, as well as unaesthetic aspects of the environment such as noise pollution. The unity of our makeup is analogous to two mirrors: what one picks up (e.g. the psyche) is reflected in the other (the body or soma), and vice versa. Hence, every phenomenon in the human system, whether harmonious or disharmonious in character, is psychosomatic.

Up until recently, Western medicine has been organized around the idea that physical illness is caused primarily by physical factors with the result that treatment has been primarily by physical means, i.e. surgery and chemotherapy. Currently, the evidence is mounting that the psyche and spirit can play a dominant role not only in the origin of illness and in its duration but also in the healing process.

John Carmody, author of several books on both Western and Eastern spirituality, writes in *Holistic Spirituality* (Paulist Press, 1983, p. 71) about the evolution, at least in some parts of the health-care community, of a new paradigm, called holistic medicine. Among its characteristics are:

- trying to care for the physical, mental, and spiritual aspirations of its patients (looking upon them as wholes);
- trying to treat people as individuals, with unique genetic, biological, and psychosocial endowments;
- trying to take into account a patient's particular culture, family context, and local community;
- looking upon health as a positive state, rather than as the absence of disease;
- emphasizing the promotion of health and the prevention of disease, stressing people's personal responsibility for their health;
- trying to help patients mobilize their capacities for healing themselves, without denying the need on occasion for dramatic interventions such as surgery;
- stressing education and self-care;

- being open to a variety of diagnostic methods and interpretational systems;
- encouraging physical, "hands on" contact between physicians and patients;
- emphasizing good nutrition and vigorous exercise;
- appreciating the positive place of sensuousness and sexuality;
- trying to make illness an opportunity for discovery;
- trying to raise the quality of each phase of a person's life;
- appreciating the setting in which health or disease is occurring, and so encouraging intimate home or hospice sites for care;
- trying to understand and change the socioeconomic conditions that perpetuate ill health;
- and changing the views of medical practitioners away from the prevailing narrowness.

There is a happy confluence between this holistic orientation to health care and the holistic Christian spirituality that is being articulated more and more today. Both stress taking into account the full range of data or influences and being sensitive to the interconnectedness of the different dimensions of the human person. As Carmody notes, where holistic medicine stresses the person's wellness, Christian spirituality places the accent upon the centrality of God's gracious love. These two stresses are by no means mutually exclusive. A generous theology of grace (read: Holy Spirit) sees the inspiration of humane movements such as holistic medicine as coming from the Spirit. Similarly, holistic medicine does not rule out the ultimacy of divine mystery.

The unity and health of mind and body was the idea that inspired physical education in ancient Greece and the development of the body among the Jews. In its early history, Christianity shared these views. Very soon, however, under the influence of neo-Platonism, there developed an excessive distrust and suspicion of the human body. Agnostic and Manichaean tendencies turned this distrust into disdain. The body, the principle of evil, became the enemy of the soul, to be combatted. The original, biblical view of the human person as a unified being became entangled with conceptions hostile to the body, as exemplified in some of the writings of St. Augustine. Christianity has thus for centuries been in the difficult position of trying to affirm the goodness of creation without delighting in human bodiliness.

Happily, Christian spokespersons are today rejecting this mind/body dualism. Leo Suenens, retired Cardinal Archbishop of Malines-Bruxelles, said in his opening address to a scientific Congress convoked in Munich in 1972 by the Olympic organizing committee: "Christian thought, if I may be so bold as to say so, has sided with the human condition. It no longer wants anything to do with the spirituality that sees the body as the prison of the soul. Its concern extends not merely to the soul, but to the human person as a total reality. Christ is not only the life of the soul, but the life of the whole human person. The whole takes first place, rather than the parts. The human person is neither a soul and a body, nor a soul with a duplicate body, but rather inspirited flesh and an enfleshed spirit. One *is* one's body and *is* one's soul, at one and the same time."

Wellness and Spirituality

"In addition to viewing human life as a total system," writes Dick Anderson in "A Holistic View of Health: A Search for Systemic Harmony" (*Holistic Health Lifebook,* And/Or Press, Berkeley, 1981, pp. 9–10), "the new theory of health commits itself explicitly to certain beliefs. The first is that the essence of the individual is spirit. . . ."

Yet it must be said that many of the wellness writers and promoters pay no serious attention to the spiritual aspect of the human person. When the word *spiritual* is used, it is often with reference to the *psychological,* or to an invisible bond that connects all living beings. In the above article, Dick Anderson's explanation of what he means by spirit is a good example: "That is, that each individual can be and needs to be part of an increasingly caring community that includes all other life, and especially other human beings." There is still no explicit reference to the Ground of all being, to the Source of life, to God.

As a biblical scholar, John J. Pilch discerned a clear relationship between notions of wellness and concepts in the Jewish and Christian traditions. Not finding this directly addressed in any wellness literature, he set out to relate religion to wellness in a complete fashion that would embrace the totality of human life, integrating religious practices and viewpoints into a distinctive wellness-promoting life-style. In the spirituality of Judaism he finds key links. It is the breath, the spirit of God, that is the source and permanence of human life. Life is a gift from God, a share in God's own life. As such, life is a treasure to be cherished, nourished, and enhanced.

When one considers that the wellness philosophy seeks to bring one from death-dealing patterns to life-affirming patterns, one has put a finger upon a theme that is at the very heart of both Jewish and Christian spirituality: the passage from death to life, understood either in terms of the exodus or in terms of the death and resurrection of Jesus. The paschal theme is so inherently and integrally *there* in wellness concepts that it is surprising to find so little reflection and development given to spirituality in most wellness literature. Spiritual values and religious beliefs provide some of the strongest motives for revising a health-destructive life-style or, for that matter, strengthening a life-affirming one. Hence, Pilch's definition is: "an ever-expanding experience of pleasurable and purposeful living which you and I, especially as motivated by spiritual values and religious beliefs, create and direct for ourselves in any way we choose."

In the next chapter, I will try to give a more concerted development to the spiritual component of wellness by proposing a spirituality for wellness. Since in the last half of this book we are going to consider several fitness activities in direct relation to "the spiritual life," it is essential that we first get a good grasp of the points at which fitness and spirituality interconnect and ultimately converge.

The early Fathers of the Church, in reflecting on the Word of God becoming flesh, observed that "Whatever is received is received according to the mode of the receiver." "The receiver" of that revelation today spends a lot of time and energy running, dancing, skiing, playing tennis, football, basketball and soccer. If God's revelation to us is to be received and integrated into our lives today, it must be able to be identified and appreciated in the midst of our preoccupations. Isaac Hecker, founder of the Paulist Fathers, the first religious community of men founded in this North American context, once preached: "We must be able to find Christ here and now, in this day and age, or he is no Christ, no savior for us."

Granted, seeking to integrate spirituality and sports would not be important outside of a cluster of easeful lands where the recreational experience is wildly popular. We cannot deny that this is a discussion which would little interest, for example, the people of Lebanon who run for their lives and listen not for a starter's gun but for a sniper's. Yet, that is not our context. In North America, we run for fun and fitness. Instead of feeling guilty about that, instead of perceiving it only as a luxury of the affluent, why not uncover the deepest and most positive dimensions inherent in our human activity and, in the spirit of Paul's letter to the Colossians, "dedicate ourselves to thankfulness" (3:15)?

To look at your life through the lenses offered here may enable you to see your sports activities as a gateway through which you can embark on a conscious and positive development of the life-enhancing potential available to you through a spirituality that prizes your bodily experiences. It can also add another dimension to your appreciation of those "breakthrough" experiences which you may personally know in running or swimming or skiing. This framework of philosophical and religious principles and convictions, rooted in and flowing from human experience, invites you to see your sporting hours as a foretaste of the kind of harmonious, satisfying, fulfilling living which is our Creator's offer to and dream for us.

Chapter 2

A Spirituality for Wellness

"The end of life is life: life in its fullness, life in its richness, life in abundance."

Francis Baur
in *Life in Abundance*

In the past several years I have met any number of people who have distanced themselves from the Church because they felt that they were too full of the zest for life, too sensual, too sexual and generally too human and complicated to live the spiritual life.

Most often the complaint sounds something like this: "I can never be a really spiritual person. I am just too restless! I want to live too much! I am too full of life! I want to experience things more! I am just too unspiritual!"

Such an attitude, while extremely common, is dangerous. When in fact someone in all sincerity believes that he or she is too full of life and eros, restlessness and complexity to live the spiritual life, that person is being sucked in by a viral heresy which would have us believe that eros, the drive for life, is fundamentally irreligious. Eros is the very basis of the spiritual life and everyone, absolutely everyone, must live a spiritual life.

What we do with the eros inside of us, be it heroic or perverse, is directly related to our spiritual life. The tragedy is that so many persons, full of riches and bursting with life, see this drive as something which is essentially irreligious, as something which sets them against what is spiritual. Nothing could be further from the truth. Our erotic impulses are God's lure in us. We experience them precisely as "spirit," as that which makes us more than mere mammals.

However, again and again, in my ministry and in my friendships I am confronted with persons who sincerely believe that they are unspiritual when in fact they are deeply spiritual persons. Because they have not found a "spirituality" which enables them to integrate their drive for life, celebration and sexuality into a commitment which includes Christian sexual morality, prayer and involvement with a Eucharistic community, they are forced into a false dilemma. They feel they must choose between a Christian commitment (which appears as erotic suicide) and a life partially away from Christian community, sacraments, prayer and morality, but within which they feel they can be fully human, sensual, sexual and celebrating.

This dilemma, within which the Church is seen as a parasite, sucking life's pulse out of its subjects, then allows society's amorality to parade itself as being ultimately life-giving and the true defender of eros.

A perfect example of this is seen in Mary Gordon's poignant novel, *Final Payments*. Her heroine, Isabelle Moore, is a very bright, talented, deep and frustrated person who has to choose constantly between faith-God-Church and her tremendous passion for life, celebration and sexuality. Poor Isabelle can see no room to express her passion within the confines of a religious commitment. So she is forced to abandon her religious practices and all links to Church in an effort to find passion and full life in celebrating life and sexuality with her non-Christian friends.

Isabelle, like so many of us, misunderstood her passion and drive for life as something essentially non-religious. That forced upon her this illicit dichotomy. Few things are hurting us as badly at present as that misconception because what it does is identify the spiritual life with piety, naiveté, lack of sensuality and sexuality, lack of passion, and lack of interest in, and zest for, life itself.

Such an attitude serves to block any deep journey toward the type of love, friendship, sexual integration and Christian commitment that could bring one genuine life. It hides the true meaning of our drive for life and becomes an excuse to selfishly pursue pleasure and to refuse to prioritize a relationship with God and community.

This is a plea: if you are the type of person who understands yourself as too complicated, too bursting with eros, too driven in the pursuit of life, too sensual and too sexual to be a real spiritual person—then don't, please don't, see this drive as something irreligious. Nobody is more qualified than you, nor more called, to live the spiritual life. Moreover, only in the spiritual life will that spirit with all its noble and lusty impulses find peace and fulfillment.

Those who, like my sister-in-law, respond passionately to the serene beauty of the lake country; who are ready on short notice for new adventures of travel and learning; who know regularly the exhilaration of a refreshing swim, a downhill flight on skis, an early morning run; who love to dance and appreciate good food—those are precisely the ones *most* suited to be intimates with the Lord of Life.

Under their passion and striving and enjoyment lies a very real spirituality, though they may have considered it too body-oriented or too this-worldly to call it such.

The Fleshiness of It All: Spirituality for Bodyspirits

We are uncomfortably aware today that there is not one single worldview, but many. My travels in the East have been enormously enriching, most of all because they have immersed me in another worldview. My dialogue with the growing Islamic population in North America makes me aware of their outlook. And the claims being tendered by the native peoples of this continent to the respective governments make me aware of yet another perspective and experience. Each time I step within one of these worldviews and look at the world through these new lenses, I cannot trivialize them in a patronizing way by saying they are "true" or "false." Each one renders service, helps the one who is raised within that worldview to hold his or her experience together in a meaningful way.

In each of these worldviews the term spirituality has different levels of meaning. Yet it is not without an underlying, unifying bond: spirituality has to do with the way we live our lives, and that holds true whatever worldview one stands within. The controlling concern of our respective spiritual quests is what enables us to live our lives in the here and now in the most fulfilling way. What values will motivate us?

Formerly the word spirituality meant having to do with our "spiritual" life or life of private prayer with God. The basic premise underlying this concept was that the way we grow holier is by our personal prayer-life. Spiritual books dealt with the topic of prayer and spiritual things meant a set of values and realities outside the ordinary realm of human experience.

Today, however, we have broadened our grasp of what it means to grow in holiness. There are probably two major causes contributing to this: what we have learned about the seamless unity of our being from human psychology and our renewed interest in the Bible as a source of understanding of what it means to be holy. Today we recognize that there isn't any distinction between "spiritual" growth and human growth. They are the same reality. My growing closer to God (who is Love) is holiness, and as I grow as a loving and caring person, I am growing in holiness. Prayer is important because it puts me in direct contact with God, the source of my growth, but it is just one of the ways in which I grow in holiness. I also grow through self-discovery and interaction with others. I grow through the experience of struggle and pain and loss. It is this total reality of the growth experience which is referred to today when we speak of "holiness" or "spirituality."

The very word "holy" has in the past evoked for us spectres of gaunt people leading a life stripped of human joy. Whatever the religious cultures of other ages required of their saints, we today instinctively reject a holiness that calls us to become spirit rather than men and women of inspirited-flesh.

But where do we find the spiritual masters to accompany us pilgrims of the twentieth and twenty-first centuries? Where do we go for spiritual resources? A brief survey of the religious book section in most bookstores will reveal new additions of spiritual classics made readily accessible in paperback. Names such as Gregory of Nyssa, Julian of Norwich, Teresa of Avila, Meister Eckhart, Jakob Boehme, John of the Cross, Catherine of Siena, John Wesley, George Fox, Francis and Clare, Gregory Palamas and others lie before us as an ecumenical treasure as well as an authentic symbol of human and religious unity.

But what should we seek from these saints? Imitations? Consolation? Ideas? We do not wish to try to recreate the past. The answer, I think, is that we simply go to these classics to put ourselves in touch with the concrete, lived event of holiness. Tell us your story, we plead with them. Let us be burned by the fire of the Living God that consumed those who saw all of life as a threshold to the dwelling place of the Gracious One who rules the universe while yet being very close to it. We want to taste the ecstatic joy of people who led full lives and somehow saw their pain and loneliness, their success and failure blossom into a fulfillment beyond expectation. Tell us of your dark nights, your political struggles with structures and institutions, your agony to find human words to describe the inexpressible. We sense you are like us, despite the mystery that surrounds you. Share with us! What is your secret?

So we climb the mountain of their works to commune with them and hear their story. And when we descend from our communication with them, we realize that it has served to make us more aware that we have the resources already within us for that which we seek.

The spiritual path we venture along will be ultimately our own. When do I become the real Tom or Suzanne or Kevin or

Donna? How will my story unfold? Can I really trust my experience?

There is an old word translated from the Latin of scholastic theology which has not yet outlived its usefulness: connaturality. Technical and impersonal though it may sound, the word has a meaning full of the warm breath of human life. To say that God or holiness is connatural to us implies that our spiritual quest need not lead us away from ourselves to the rarefied air of gothic heights, or to the rigors of an inhuman asceticism. Rather, the holy is a dimension of our everyday lives. As we work, enjoy, make friends and pursue life together, a loving presence accompanies us—call it grace or God—a presence which struggles to come to birth and mature in our lives. Thus, spirituality becomes a style of discernment, developing the vision to perceive the deeper movement of life, the divine milieu which permeates our every day. We need only the courage to embrace our experience, to live our story, trusting that the unfolding events will in time shape us into a self which is full, authentic, holy. This is the true meaning of the word asceticism: the artful fashioning of something beautiful for God.

The questions which trace our spiritual path are not unknown to us, though we may not have recognized them as signposts of the *spiritual* life. How do we learn to read God's presence in our life experience? What does our sexuality, that ambivalent, yet powerfully creative dynamic, reveal about our process of holiness? What is birthing in ourselves and others through our relationships with family, friends, and everyday acquaintances? What is the source of the compassion which sometimes wells up in us? These questions seek not mere information but to discern an inner movement, an emerging Presence.

We must live these questions out in the only life we know: the one that we live in this flesh, with these needs, these passions, and these possibilities. On one level, Christian spirituality is the experience of the continual gift of Christ to those united to him in the Holy Spirit, as well as a fidelity which must constantly be re-newed since it is always being tested by the circumstances of life and human history. On another, broader level, my spirituality is my stance toward the world in view of this experience of gift, a stance characterized by certain attitudes and convictions. What has been pivotal in my own way of seeing reality is that I have come to understand myself and the world in which I live in the ultimate context of God.

The Why of It All: More And Fuller Life

How did I arrive at this understanding? The starting point was that I was alive and loved. The gradual discovery was that the main instruments I had to work with were this spirited flesh and these loves. In the Scripture stories of the Bible I saw people seeking ever fuller life with passion and intensity: Noah trying to sur-vive; Abraham and Sarah seeking to enrich their life by handing it on to children; Moses leading the people toward the promised land; David risking to give his people security and safety; and most of all, Jesus, proclaiming "I have come that you may have life, and have it more abundantly" (John 10:10). The message came through: life and life alone is what we live for, and there is no substitute for the fullness of life itself. Its passion and intensity is its own reward, and I should not allow myself to stop short and be satisfied with medals, degrees, clippings, an executive posi-tion, six-figure salary or any other of life's assurances and idols. This is the first fundamental affirmation: *the passion and intensity of life is essentially its own and the primary reward.*

Corollary to this fundamental affirmation is that what life is essentially about is the quest for more and fuller life. And life to the full, both ultimately and here and now, is only to be experienced in the context of God, the source of all life. One's spirituality will be judged, then, by the passion of one's quest for abundant life and one's perseverance in the face of all odds. To say that our spiritual quest is to live our lives as richly and fully and intensely as is possible risks sounding like the theme of the me-generation all over again. The critical difference is that the enrichment of our lives is directly linked, not just to the relationships available to us, but to *what we pursue, choose, and value in those relationships.*

We are faithful, first of all, not to something outside of ourselves, but to our own integrity and authenticity. Our struggle is not a competition for prestige but for the quality of life itself.

Perhaps this version of the spiritual quest strikes us as too egocentric, too "natural." But what else could we possibly wish to be if we did not wish to be humanly fulfilled? Is there any fulfillment besides human fulfillment open to us? What else could I wish to be other than humanly satisfied?

If "supernatural" means beyond the natural, then I must honestly admit that I don't know what that means. I only have this flesh, this personal life, these loves. The message of the Incarnation, the implications from which we shall reflect upon further in a moment, surely seems to indicate that the process of human fulfillment begins within this world where the very stuff of our perfection is the daily interchange with other fleshed lives.

The first time that someone suggested to me that the final end of this world might not be the destruction of all life but the bringing to fullness of that life in an entirely new form of existence, I began to perceive differently the perfection to which the Scriptures call us. Rather than seeing it in relation to something other and different from this life, it began to refer to more and fuller life that I live here and now. In this scheme of things, the perfection of life does not mean the ending of life or the shift to a different kind of existence but simply *more life.*

In what does "more life" consist? St. John's answer:

> This is eternal life:
> to *know* Jesus Christ,
> and God who sent him. (17:3)

In other words, those who "*know* Jesus Christ" and are in relationship with him are already living eternal, infinite life. The deeper and more intimate the relationship, the "more life" there is. Heaven, or union with God, then, is our very lives, freed from the debilitating shackles of selfishness and sin, and raised to an intensity and fullness approaching that of the very life of God who is the source of all life. The qualities which we have zealously nurtured blossom into fullness. Recall the parable in Luke 19:11 of the sums of money: "Whoever has will be given more, but the one who has not will lose the little he has."

When Jesus says that he came that we might have life and have it to the full, there is no mention of saving our souls or bringing us to the beatific vision. If we are to take that seriously, we may have to trade in our notion of heaven-as-reward and accept the idea that our real reward is the knowledge that we have accepted God's gift of life and responded to it with passion and with intensity. If the end of life is the enhancement of life itself, then the satisfied will be those who have sought not safety but sanctity, who have risked their security and timidity to strike into the deep in the only cause worthwhile: the cause of more and fuller life. The purpose of our existence will not then be viewed as some reward tacked on to the end of our lives. It is the life I live here and now, in this time and place, with these particular people.

If the abundance of life is the goal of both our human and our religious striving, then we have to be concerned about discovering the possibilities of life in abundance; we will have to be ready to invest some time and energy in pursuing the conditions for abundant life so as to experience for ourselves the qualities of enhanced living. How do we grow in our appreciation for life? How do we enjoy? How do we seek fulfillment? These are not irrelevant questions. They are the very reason why a book on spirituality and sports is worth the time and energy it takes to write it.

It may seem strange to some to address such subjects while the world totters on the brink of nuclear disaster and millions upon millions are starving. Yet there are also millions upon millions who daily invest enormous amounts of psychic and physical energy and time into running and skiing and dancing and playing tennis and team sports. They are not going to stop doing so because nuclear arms proliferate or because governments cannot organize themselves to get the world surplus food to those who need it most. If nothing else, these pages seek to take certain people—those in the "affluent Western world" interested either in sports or spirituality, or both—where they're at and invite them to maximize their investment of time and energy. If life is worth living, it's worth living to the full.

Whatever God's purposes are with us, God is using the conditions and concrete relationships of our lives, the things we do each day and all the available possibilities open to us to enhance our lives. Rather than inviting us to lay away insurance for some future life, God invites us to relate positively to *all* the conditions of our lives now—children, studies, job, recreation, prayer, friends, community service—as the stuff of our relationship with the Divine. Whatever touches life and living, the Source of all life is there, saying, "I come that you might have life and have it to the full."

The Wonder of It All: God Is Love

The kingdom of God is not a place; it is an experience.

The second fundamental affirmation which provides the motivation and the content of our spiritual quest is that *God is love* (1 John 4:8) *and holds all our living as precious and dear.*

After affirming that everything called into being was good, God turned it over to Adam and Eve as though it were tailor-made for their delight. The world in the Genesis account comes off as eminently hospitable, sustaining, life-giving, and affording enormous satisfaction. Scientific and philosophical thinkers today who propose that the entire network of cosmic reality is knit to-

gether and somehow "feels" find their paradigm in our progenitors. Fashioned from stuff of the earth, they fed off the world,
seeking the fullness of human life in harmony with all the members of the created realm who, it might be said, were seeking essentially the same thing: quality and intensity of life. In their
humanness, our progenitors were of both earth and of God—and
of supreme value to each.

The fall does not belong at center stage in the creation story,
but somewhere in the wings. The main point of this story is that
we are invited to recover the gracious and harmonious relationships which characterized our beginnings and toward which we
journey as our final end.

The intuition of creation-centered theology, as articulated for
example in Matthew Fox's book, *Original Blessing* (Bear & Company, Santa Fe, N.M.), is the affirmation of both the goodness of
the world and the goodness of human life precisely because both
are essentially related to God. Therefore the bottom line is not sin,
not depravity, not the curse, but the saving grace offered by the
God of life whose very nature is nothing else but love and who
leaves enough clues so that those who seek with a pure and per-
severing heart will find their way back to their proffered inheritance of goodness and beauty.

The theme that is sounded time and again in the Old Testament is the mighty struggle to bring life to its full potential in the
face of repeated failure. Then came that special one, Jesus, who
called God *Abba,* Father, laying claim to intimacy with the Source
of all life as our natural right and insisting with his life that God
is love.

How God is, we find in Jesus. His stories revealed him cap-
tivated by earthly detail because it was precisely here, in this
earthly environment, that his personal intuition sensed the pervasive presence of God. The stuff of Jesus' stories—flowers, wid-
ows, trees, fathers, sheep, farmers, shepherds and many others—
spoke to his heart with the voice of God and represented, not *signs*

of the activity of God but the *very activity of God* engaged in and loving every detail of life in this his own.

When Jesus saw the blind, the paralyzed and the deaf being brought to him from all directions, he trembled from within and experienced their pains in his own heart (Matthew 14:14). When he noticed that the thousands who had followed for days were tired and hungry, he said, "I am moved with compassion" (Mark 8:2). And so it was with the two blind men who called after him (Matthew 9:27), the leper who fell to his knees in front of him (Mark 1:41), and the widow of Nain who is burying her only son (Luke 7:13). They moved him, they made him feel with all his intimate sensibilities the depth of their sorrow.

His cures were a natural expression of his being our God. The mystery of God's love is not that he takes our pains away, but that he first wants to share them with us. Out of this divine solidarity comes new life. The truly good news is that God is not a distant God, a God to be feared and avoided, a God of revenge, but a God who is moved by our pains and participates in the fullness of the human struggle.

We cannot emphasize enough that when Jesus calls God his Father, he speaks about a love that includes and transcends all the love we know. It is the love of a father, but also of a mother, brother, sister, friend and lover. It is severe yet merciful, jealous yet sharing, prodding yet guiding, challenging yet caring, disinterested yet supportive, selfless yet very intimate. The many kinds of love we have experienced in our various human relationships are fully represented in the love between Jesus and his heavenly Father, but also fully transcended by this same love.

Our everyday lives are full of the kinds of relationships which Jesus describes in his stories. I need not look beyond the network of people with whom I live and move each day to find the holy ground of my meeting place with God. The godly activities to which the stories invite us will be our own contemporary parallel to the father's response to his child even in the middle of the night, to the shepherd who knows each of his sheep by name, or to the widow concerned for something as seemingly expendable as a lost coin. Such relationships of care, compassion, love and commitment are available to us all. Well within our grasp, these quiet virtues possess a sacred ability to inspire intensity and depth of response in the most ordinary of lives.

What I write of the love of God, the quality of the experience of life to which God calls us, and the possibility of mirroring God's way with us in our relationships with each other—all of this seems eminently real and immediate to me in this present moment. I have come to my parents' home on a hill that overlooks a lake through the woods to do this writing. The harmony that I experience with them; their palpable love for each other and for me; my mother's relaxed playfulness; the silent symphony of light playing upon the leaves; the serene surface of the lake; the astonishing colors of the forest creatures—red-headed woodpecker, Baltimore oriole, blue jay, gold finch, hummingbird; the many textures from rabbit's tail to treebark; the warmth of the sun; the coolness of the breeze: all dissolve together into an experience of overwhelming gift offered in tantalizing mystery by a gracious Presence.

Does that sound maudlin? What's the difference between that and Jesus seeing the gracious presence of God in the blossoming fig tree, in the mustard seed, in the wheat, and finally in the bread? It's the same world. Is it that our sensibilities are dulled in comparison with his? Or is it that the entire universe is created anew within the vision of faith? A creation-centered spirituality invites us to focus on what is there and available to everyone, everywhere, and to dedicate all our heart's energies to discovering and deepening our awareness of that gracious Presence since it is this relationship that is the most creative and fulfilling of all relationships.

And the initiative for this relationship is not just from our side. Our Scriptures and our Tradition are full of indicators that this relationship is reciprocal. The language of our prayer is that of one person speaking to another. And from the prophets comes passionate testimony that the communication is two-way: God wants, God asks, God forgives, God plans, God loves, God intends.

If we are to take seriously the language of God "wanting" and "intending" and "loving," we must be ready to grant that there is a state of affairs in the world which is not yet actualized but in which God has a real stake and is therefore very involved in seeing it reach its potential.

What is true of the world in general would be true of each of us in particular. God has a stake in how you and I turn out. If that seems far-fetched, you haven't read the prophets. If you want just a quick taste, Jeremiah 2:1–5 will do. The religious language of God being angry and forgiving, of loving and pleading conveys that God is very much affected, that God is deeply involved in what's going on precisely because every bit of it makes a difference to God. As Francis Baur puts it in *Life in Abundance: A Contemporary Christian Spirituality* (Paulist Press, 1983):

> Therefore the question is: What does God have at stake in the universe? Why would the universe, and we ourselves, make any difference to God? The reason that Scripture propounds and which our religious intuition affirms is that God has at stake the quality of his own experience. Too long has theology neutralized God, deeming God so independent and self-sufficient that nothing could disturb this infinite tranquility. If the God of Scripture is anything, he surely is not the tranquil one. Prophet after saint after mystic drive home the point that the God of our worship is the God passionately involved in the affairs of his creatures. And the sole justifying reason for this involvement is the quality of that very passion. What God has at stake in the universe is the quality of his own experience. Dare we be so obtuse as to think that the incarnation and the redemption made no difference to God? . . .

You and I have an everlasting and immeasurable impact on the love of God. The very passion of the involvement of God in human affairs testified by the prophets bespeaks the thirst of God for an intensity of experience not dependent on his will alone (pp. 90–91).

What God is doing is simply being God, that is to say, loving, deeply and intensely. As we know, genuine lovers devote themselves to discovering the infinite variety of ways in which love can be enhanced and expressed. That is how lovers create a quality of experience in their relationship which makes them want to spend more and more time together. If we were to take seriously that we are the wooed in the Song of Songs and that God is the wooer, we would derive some small insight as to just how important we and our response are to God.

Virtually the only thing that I can achieve for myself in this existence is the quality of my experiencing. And the quality of my experiencing is directly related to my perceptions or vision of the world. By some delightful arrangement, could the only gift I can offer be precisely the gift God wants—quality of experience, of relationship?

''God is love'' is the conviction that drives and sustains my faith. It is precisely this that causes me to believe that God rejoices at my ecstasy, grieves at my loss, and empathizes with my suffering. This is the understanding of God and our inter-relationship that underlay the first sermon of Dr. William Sloane Coffin Jr. after the accidental death of his son whose car broke through the guard rails of a bridge and plunged into Boston harbor:

> The night after Alex died, I was sitting in the living room of my sister's house outside of Boston when the front door opened and in came a nice-looking middle-aged woman carrying 18 quiches. When she saw me she shook her head, then headed for the kitchen, saying sadly over her shoulder, ''I just don't understand the will of God.''

Instantly I was up and in hot pursuit, swarming over her. "I'll say you don't, lady!" I said. (I knew the anger would do me good, and the instruction to her was long overdue.)

I continued, "Do you think it was the will of God that Alex never fixed that lousy windshield wiper of his, that he was probably driving too fast in such a storm, that he probably had had a couple of 'frosties' too many? Do you think it is God's will that there are no street lights along that stretch of road, and no guard rail separating the road and Boston harbor?"

Nothing infuriates me so as the incapacity of seemingly intelligent people to get it through their heads that God doesn't go around this world with his finger on steering wheels. God is against unnatural deaths. And Christ spent an inordinate amount of time delivering people from paralysis, insanity, leprosy, and muteness.

There are, of course, nature-caused deaths that are untimely and slow and pain-ridden and hard to understand. But violent deaths, such as the one Alex died—to understand those is a piece of cake. As his younger brother put it simply, standing at the head of the casket at the Boston funeral: "You blew it, buddy. You blew it."

The one thing that should never be said when someone dies is, "It is the will of God." Never do we know enough to say that. My consolation lies in knowing that it was not the will of God that Alex died; that when the waves closed over the sinking car, God's was the first of all our hearts to break.

The spiritual life has essentially to do with an awareness how important our lives and all that we do are to God.

The Unbelievableness of It All:
Love Becomes One of Us

We evidently needed some effective convincing with regard to our own inestimable value. That perhaps is what influenced John the evangelist in his Gospel prologue to choose the unique phrasing that the Word of God became, not a human being, not even a human person, but *flesh*. The expression is both graphic and dramatic. God becomes one of us, a living being of flesh and blood, experiencing life in this world just as we experience it.

It was not a masquerade party or play-acting. It was not something which could ever be taken back or undone. It was, we might say, a serious commitment. Had *our* evaluation of the world been God's, it might never have happened. But God sees more clearly than we do that all life is holy and that the body is truly the temple of the spirit. In the face of our devaluations of the flesh that embodies God and the earth which is God's home, God sent us a message: henceforth, *God is identified with and discovered within this bodiliness, this fleshiness, this materiality, this sensuality, this worldliness, this passion.*

If ever we wanted to trade in this bodily existence for another kind, in the face of that message we no longer have any grounds to do so. Where we are and what we are is now the intimate habitat of God. If ever we approached life in this world as a second-rate adventure in the service of another world, the Incarnation demands that we revise that assessment in favor of recognizing the inherent value of our embodied earthly life. In Baur's words:

> It is not so much that the Word entered into the world; it is rather that the Word *became flesh*. However much we may wish to protect the dignity and abstract purity of the Godhead, this much at least we are permitted to say: in the Incarnation, Jesus in his flesh took the world as part of himself. . . . The world quite literally became the Body of God. Ever afterward

we have no right to dismiss this world as some second-rate
practice field for the real life in heaven. The Incarnation states
that there is no practice and nothing is second-rate; life in this
world is the life of the Godhead. (pp. 84–85)

There was a time in my life when I was careless about fas-
tening seat belts or when flying in an airplane I regarded the possibility of a crash with cool detachment. ''I'll just arrive that much
quicker at the bigtime where it really counts'' ran my thoughts.
But the more I grow in a worldview which takes seriously the
meaning of the Incarnation, the more I want to live in this very
habitat which God has now made home. The more what God has
done in becoming flesh penetrates my consciousness, the more I
appreciate and understand and am sympathetic to the tenacity with
which my 90 year old grandmother clings to life, wanting the dig-
nity of living in her own home, the pleasure of tending her flowers, the creative satisfaction of preparing her meals, and the
challenge of shoveling the snow from her sidewalks. She, like
Thoreau in going to Walden Pond, wants to drink deeply from
life's cup so that when she arrives at the end of her days she will
not discover that she has not *lived*.

Last summer my sister came to Montreal to spend a week
with me. One Sunday afternoon we were walking around Beaver
Lake on the top of Mount Royal, and sat down on the grass by the
water to listen to a woodwind quartet making their open air mel-
ody for the sheer pleasure of it. Consciously savoring my sister's
presence, the glorious day, the harmonious music, and the light
dancing upon the water, I leaned against my sister's shoulder and
whispered to her: ''Sometimes the experience of life is so precious
it brings tears to my eyes.'' She nodded understandingly, and I
knew she was feeling the same sacredness.

Later that day as she was asking me to tell her what the
months ahead held for me, I hesitated, responding that sometimes
I almost feel guilty about the opportunities for interesting travel

that my work affords me because I know that many other people would like to have similar opportunities but do not. "No," she said, "don't feel that way. Go. Experience. Learn. Enjoy. If you were to pass up some opportunities because not everybody has them, then everybody loses. If those who have the opportunities to deepen and broaden their experience do so, when they come back they are more interesting people for all of us and enhance the quality of all our lives." A godly response! The point of life's journey is not just the destination, but also the quality of the traveling.

Baur writes of how our embodied lives are the context and the stuff of our spiritual journeying:

> The journey of these embodied cells is the passionate struggle to seek out the deepest qualities of life itself, to be challenged by commitment and seek after ideals which constantly lure us away from our standing path or from our lack of daring. It is the struggle to taste of life so fully that we begin to have an inkling of that fullness of life which is the Godhead. We have been told that not the lukewarm but the passionate will find their God. . . . If we are somehow shocked by Jesus' obvious this-worldly love, we have the pale consolation of knowing that he was faulted for being rather casual about fasting and penance. His words expressed during the agony in the garden are perhaps the most tender and passionate testimony about how dearly he loved this life and how unwilling he was to leave this world. The Resurrection is striking witness that his this-world loyalty was not misplaced. (pp. 85–86)

If we wish to devise a spirituality for ourselves whereby the spiritual-minded must be other-worldly and whereby spiritual growth is measured by an antipathy toward this world, this body, this life, then we will have to fly in the face of the very example God has given us. The ways in which we manage to discount God's "modeling behavior" are subtle and pervasive. On the one

hand, for example, Jesus gives us as his new commandment that
we love one another as he has loved us. On the other hand, many
of us have been made to fear in different ways that our deep love
for another could somehow deter and perhaps even disbar us from
the kingdom where love is all in all. We have not been burdened
with this world and this flesh in order that we might weasel our
way out. Rather, we have been gifted with this world and these
bodies because this is where God dwells. All flesh is holy and the
ground of all human endeavors is sacred. It is in these bodies that
we work out our salvation.

The central concern of spirituality is fullness of life. Since
the only life we know is earthly and sensual, it follows that this is
the stuff of our spirituality. Hence, even such things as running
and jumping and skiing and swimming can become part of our
language with God. The challenge of any spirituality is to integrate all the aspects of life in our engagement with the world. We
arrive at wholeness by using to the fullest the stuff of our human
experience, rather than by denying or diminishing it or seeing it
as outside the pale of our relationship with God.

The Sinfulness of Us All:
How Badly Are We Crippled?

The Paulist Fathers' novitiate sits in the wooded hills of
northeastern New Jersey on a gentle knoll that slopes down
through the trees to a placid lake. The chapel wing of the building
extends toward the lake so that those assembled are looking in the
direction of this tranquil scene. There is just one small difficulty:
the wall behind the altar is solid stone. I have yet to meet the person who does not visit that chapel and remark, ''How beautiful it
would be if that wall were glass and the creation were allowed to
come in.''

The stone wall, however, was a conscious decision by the
novice master at the time of the building's construction. He didn't

want those gathered for prayer to be distracted. He represented
another worldview, another spirituality.

The more intensely we come to know and experience the
world, wrote the Jesuit paleontologist Teilhard de Chardin (d.
1955), the closer we come to God. The entire universe is one "divine milieu." We attain an experience of God not, as the traditional ascetical writers of the nineteenth century argued, primarily
through purgation, contemplation, and mystical union, but rather
we encounter God by turning toward the things of the earth in love
and reverence. The natural delight we take in life and in all that
exists is the first dawn of divine illumination. The great mystery
of Christianity, according to Teilhard, is not that God appears, but
that God shines through the universe. Our prayer then should be
that we might see God in all things. There is more than a trace of
Franciscan spirituality in Teilhard's sense of the presence of God
in the physical universe and in his sense of the activating energy
of Christ, as the omega point of evolution, across the entire cosmos.

But, as one of my friends was fond of saying regarding the
body of Teilhard's thought, "there's not enough sin in it." It is
quite possible that some of you have had the same thought with
reference to these pages. Any effort to sketch out a spirituality
must at some point deal honestly with sin.

The different traditions of Christianity, in writing their line
on the subject, have placed the accent on different syllables. Eastern Orthodoxy stresses the spiritual side of human existence to
such an extent that the natural foundation is sometimes nearly lost.
Much of Protestantism has so emphasized the depravity of the natural human condition apart from the grace of God that the natural
order can only be viewed in thoroughly negative terms. While
"nature" is still largely absent from Eastern Orthodox theology
of grace and has generally been resisted by Protestant theology,
Catholicism has historically and theologically emphasized the importance of the natural and the "natural order."

In the Catholic tradition, however, the introduction of the concept of nature in the explanation of grace has at times led to a dualistic vision of human existence in relation to God. On the one hand, God is our Creator and establishes a relationship with us whereby we could, hypothetically, have a "natural end" or state of "natural happiness." On the other hand, God is our Savior through Christ, and by the grace of Christ we enter into a new relationship of communion with God in which we are transformed interiorly by the Spirit of Christ.

While we may not be very conversant with historic theologies of nature and grace, we know all too well the reality that has occasioned such reflections. We lie, we steal, we betray, we kill, we violate, and we destroy. All too often, we soil and ruin the best and finest in our relationships. Hence we dare not build theological sand castles which will be washed away by the first waves of dark reality. In whatever we say about what God has done for and in our world, we dare not deny the poisonous reality of evil. We do not need to go to Asia and Africa to find starvation and cruel poverty; we do not need to go to Central America or behind the Iron Curtain to locate torture, pain and death. They are all here, in our very midst. Each of us, in fact, has had a personal role in inflicting suffering and hurt on those around us. As Sean Fagan said in his book *Has Sin Changed?* (Michael Glazier, Inc., Wilmington, Del., 1977), "If perchance we feel guilty, we should not discount the possibility that we *feel* guilty because we *are* guilty."

In the face of all this, how is it possible that we can, without consummate idealism and naiveté, claim that life in abundance was bestowed upon us by God through Christ? How can we have a spirituality that is anything other than somber and morose? A colleague remarked recently that certain theologies tend to whitewash life's dirt and grime. I thought of his words today at the funeral of a man who hanged himself with his television cable. Fifty-five years of life on this earth, and there were just three of us there to mark his passing.

Are not the Evangelicals right in constantly opposing the spirit against the flesh and portraying our lives as a continual spiritual combat fought upon the battleground of our own selves? I doubt that there are any of us left who have not listened to the tele-evangelists present the entire cosmos and all those who people it as some vast conspiracy to lure us from our true perfection which is the pursuit of God alone. There is a cruel antagonism, we are told, between ourselves, other people, and the world; and we take perilous risks by responding to the attractions of earthly existence for they can only finally distract us from the one true beauty which is God. To listen to them is to know that this is not our home and that we are aliens on this planet.

Such spiritual pessimism succeeds in making us dig our trenches a bit deeper and strapping on our helmets more securely, but it does little to promote what Roger Schutz, the founder of Taizé, calls "the wonder of a love": God so loved this world that he sent his only-begotten Son to inhabit its earth and dwell in its flesh.

In the face of such pessimistic witness, we must go back again and again to the central and essential claim of our scriptural heritage and the early Fathers: creation is good. "The Son of God became the Son of man," said St. Athanasius, "in order that the sons of men, the sons of Adam, might be made sons of God." In the Christian East, the title "theologian" is reserved for St. John the Evangelist, St. Gregory Nazianzen and St. Symeon. All of them are exponents of this life as communion with God, represented by these words of Symeon the new theologian:

> He took upon himself my flesh
> and he gave me his Spirit.
> And I also became god by divine grace,
> the son of God but by adoption.
> Oh what dignity, what glory!

In Eastern Christian thought, all theology is mystical and its purpose is deification or divinization. The way of the knowledge of God is necessarily the way of deification. This is not some fringe sectarian belief, but a conviction absolutely central to Orthodox theology and to all Orthodox spirituality.

No, we must not gloss over the story of the fall in Genesis, but neither should we let it be lifted from its place as a sub-story and be read as the central message of the Old Testament. To do so would be to allow the story of the fall to dictate our understanding of the spiritual life and to define ourselves by sin rather than by grace. The bottom line is still Paul's: "Where sin abounds, grace does more abound."

> When we were reconciled to God by the death of his Son, we were still enemies; now that we have been reconciled, surely we may count on being saved by the life of his Son. Not merely because we have been reconciled, but because we are filled with joyful trust in God, through our Lord, Jesus Christ, through whom we have already gained our reconciliation. . . . The results of the gift also outweigh the results of one man's sin: for after one single fall came judgment with a verdict of condemnation, now after many falls comes grace with its verdict of acquittal. . . . However great the number of sins committed, grace was even greater (Romans 5:11, 16, 21).

In the light of this could we possibly think that Jesus wants us to flee the world because there is evil in it? If a cue may be drawn from his own life, the quality and meaning of our lives is to be derived, not from fleeing evil, but in the overcoming of evil. Yes, at times the evil is of frightening proportion and threatens to beat us back, but our faith is that its spine has already been broken by Christ who calls us to link hands in a partnership with the

Source of life itself toward making the abundance of life over death unmistakably clear for all those of faint heart to see.

A key sign of healthy prayer is that it should encourage us in the strong and durable love that Jesus preached.

Jesus invited people to come as free human beings and to believe that, with his grace, their feelings of fragility, vulnerability, timidity, deep-seated fear and insecurity could be confronted and healed.

Jesus proclaimed a resilient and durable faith. To a militant people he preached peacemaking. To people commanded to avoid adultery he proclaimed a new limit, to shun even lust in their hearts. To men accustomed to easy dismissal of their wives, he proclaimed permanent commitment. To people who had heard "an eye for an eye and a tooth for a tooth" he blessed a tough, non-violent meekness which offered the wicked no resistance, walked an extra mile, and loaned possessions with generosity.

Jesus challenged his followers, steeped in separation from and hostility toward other tribes, beliefs and nations, to love not only their neighbors, but to love their enemies and pray for those who persecuted them. To a people for whom wealth and possessions were a sign of God's blessings he preached poverty and security based on their trust in God.

In the Beatitudes he celebrated the poor in spirit, the gentle. He lauded those who show mercy and promised comfort to those who mourn. He blessed peacemakers and those who work for justice and are persecuted for their efforts.

To marginal people of ill-repute and supposed little worth, he proclaimed a bold message. "You are the salt of the earth," the "light of the world," "a city built on a hilltop," a "light" that must shine before people.

Jesus promised that faith would make them bold when they expected to be most fearful.

He promised, too, that they would find this way of life a

"light burden and a sweet yoke." Christ came to raise up saints from sinners, the bold from the timid, the wise from the un-learned, and martyrs from the weak. He pledged his Spirit of love to guide people willing to risk such a venture.

It is clear that Christ proclaimed a way of life which affirmed that faith can encourage little, fearful, anxious people to assume burdens, make free choices and follow a demanding way of life seemingly suited for people who are strong and durable.

Thus, any healthy spirituality for today's Christians, espe-cially in these days of struggle for justice, must nurture people in the strength and durability of Jesus' original preaching if it is to be holistic and valid.

Spiritualities that encourage fragility, timidity, fear and flight are suspect. Spiritualities which focus on "Jesus and me" can nurture for a time. But even at their best they lack the mature living of the great commandment which summons us to let our near and distant neighbors have an integral place in our hearts. At worst, they lead to spiritual selfishness and religious narcissism.

What this book is essentially about is the transformation of human consciousness toward a more constant awareness of the Holy everywhere present to us. In the language of Christian spir-ituality, as Thomas Merton once observed, one is not a contem-plative unless one embraces the political, economic, and social concerns of one's time.

The Cultivation of It All:
What Practices Should We Emphasize?

There is a tendency to see the spiritual quality of any person's life in direct proportion to the methods and techniques and disci-plines in which that person is engaged. I do not believe that spir-ituality is primarily a matter of practices, of doing things. Rather, it is a question of being aware of who we are in our relationships before God and with God. If that awareness is there, then my practices and disciplines will have meaning. I realize it is a little like the chicken and the egg question, because it is certainly those very practices which help me to cultivate and live in that awareness throughout the activities of the day.

What I want to be careful to maintain here is similar to what I have written elsewhere of fasting (*Fasting Rediscovered, A Guide to Health and Wholeness for Your Body-Spirit* (Paulist Press, 1981): all these practices are like so many means, so many instruments in the Christian toolbox. The goal is never simply the mastery of the tools, but the quality of the dwelling I can build with them. In this vein, Baur explains the word "asceticism" as denoting the *artful shaping of a material:*

> The spiritual person is ascetic precisely because the spiritual person is the one who is interested in and dedicated to the artful handling of the world, the artful shaping of one's own self, and the artful forming of one's life into something beautiful. The beautiful is the supreme attraction of the spiritual person, and hence his or her energies are committed to the creation of the beautiful in life, the beautiful in the world. The only material available for this artful shaping is life itself, and thus it is that the spiritual person takes life in hand to inform it with the transcendent beauty of God. . . . This artful fashioning of life cannot be done by coercion or regimentation; it is only achieved by virtue of spontaneous desire and passionate pursual. (pp. 256–257)

At the same time, he admits validity to the secondary sense of the term, the one with which most people may be more familiar, i.e. "the giving up of things we liked or the undergoing of hardship—all, somehow, for the love of God." What is chiefly of value in this secondary understanding is that the spiritual life does involve setting priorities whereby we forego lesser values for greater, and making choices which may involve sacrificing certain worthwhile things for the sake of supreme worth.

In the end, if what we have done or given up has not contributed toward making us warmer, simpler, gentler, more generous and compassionate, then it simply wasn't worth the time and the energy.

> This is what God asks of you,
> only this:
> to act justly,
> to love tenderly,
> and to walk humbly with your God.
> (Micah 6:8)

As far as our spiritual growth is concerned, the bigness of what we did or gave up is irrelevant—the only thing that matters is "the size of the life we have artfully fashioned." In the shaping and being shaped in our own spiritual life, we need to select those few, most beneficial exercises that will give our lives the proper malleability enabling us to be shaped according to our unique destiny.

The disciplines of the spiritual life are of immense potential value; they have earned their credibility by being of service to many people over a long period of time. But there is no reason for us to limit ourselves to the approaches of the past in enhancing the quality of our lives and in becoming more polylingual in our communication with God. There are other kinds of "exercises"—literal, physical ones—which can be usefully employed in our contemporary experience for the development of our experience of abundant life.

Sports, too, are a school of asceticism and discipline. The discipline learned in sports can act as a refining power, exercise a channeling role. Rushing waters harnessed become a source of energy: power is made available for constructive purposes.

A Response

As a recapitulation of these themes, a response to my sister-in-law's letter would look like this:

Dear Mary Claire,

Your question touches a very real chord. I'm glad you shared it because it has triggered much reflection for me, too. Some of your lines in particular stand out for me:

"When I try to incorporate a little spirituality via reading or prayer, my good intentions last only for a night or two." Perhaps the notion of spirituality could be opened up to include your awareness of God as it breaks upon you through activities to which you're more naturally attracted—like your running and your skiing. Your experience there may be the starting point from which an awareness of God as real and present to you moves out into other areas of your life—perhaps ending in an appreciation for the Bible or what is more formally called "prayer." Some people start there. Others end there. It doesn't work the same for everyone. Work with those few "exercises" or instruments which help you to artfully shape your life, which make you more peaceful, generous, and compassionate.

Try talking to the kids about the God you experience in those "most inspirational times," like your ski experience of tranquility and beauty at French Rapids. I have a hunch the children will catch a reverence, an enthusiasm, a sense of mystery from you that will give them a wonderful "taste" for God.

You refer to those moments as "great inspiration for then, but not later that night or the next day in church." That almost sounds a little greedy! Start with the rich lump that's given, and slowly, by cultivating that faculty of awareness, spread it around to other parts of your day and life.

"I can put up with sub-zero temperatures, blisters, and sore muscles, but can't follow through on Lenten goals."

Suppose you were to see your sporting activities as your spiritual (as well as your physical) exercises. Given how faithfulness to these "exercises" helps you feel positive about yourself, more patient and sensitive with the children, better able to be attentive to your husband, they are directly contributing to your ability to joyfully live your Christian vocation as a responsible woman, wife and mother. Could you ask for more from any set of "spiritual exercises"? Take the blisters and sore muscles and cold fingers as your penance if you feel you need one!

It's fairly safe to assume that your experience of God as love will come primarily through your relationships with Dan and the boys. If everything is clicking there, the potential for experience of God-as-love is all over the place. It's just a question of learning how to "read" that Presence and communicate with it naturally, spontaneously. As running and canoeing and swimming become part of your language with God, preparing meals, caring for the boys, going to church, and a night out with Dan can't be far behind. The challenge of any spirituality is to integrate *all* the aspects of life; some are undoubtedly easier than others.

I especially appreciated that part of your letter where you described an impressive discipline in your athletic activities and then end with, "but I can't make myself listen to the entire homily or ponder a short daily reading." Because I agree with you that the human qualities involved in sports are the same as those needed for the spiritual life, it isn't, I don't think, a question of "can't." The equipment is there. All that's lacking is the application. You may find it easier to concentrate in church when the boys are more grown up! The quality of the preaching or the kind of reading you're trying to do might not be making matters easier, either. Try to get a good thought or two and consider yourself normal. As the *Desiderata* says, "Beyond a wholesome discipline, be gentle with yourself."

By this time you have a pretty good idea of what my response is likely to be to your final question: "But what about my spiritual life?"

Your whole letter, as far as I can see, is about your spiritual life! The positive experience of your body that you describe is a well from which to draw your living water. God embraced that flesh and dwells in it. The more you become attuned to it, exulting in its harmony, strength, and flexibility, learning how to bear its tensions and sufferings gracefully, the more you glorify its Creator, the One who also chose it as "home."

Since I am inclined to judge spirituality by the passion of one's quest for abundant life and one's perseverance in the face of all odds, I'd have to say that anyone who juggles all the interesting pursuits you do and has the stick-to-it-tiveness of a marathoner is a choice candidate for a rich spiritual life. "Strong" and "durable" are words familiar to an athlete. They're also the qualities that characterize the followers of Jesus. Holiness is not a question of becoming something *other* than what you are, but of becoming *more* of it—in particular, more aware of the different layers of meaning of what is already there.

Your zest for living, for challenge, meaning, and new levels of experience, suggests you are eminently qualified for the spiritual life. I'll venture even further: only in cultivating this dimension of life called "spiritual" will that noble spirit of yours find peace and fulfillment.

*   *   *

Further Reading

For a fuller development of these themes, I enthusiastically refer the reader to Francis Baur's *Life in Abundance: A Contemporary Spirituality* (Paulist Press, 1983) to which I am deeply indebted in these pages.

Chapter 3

Wellness, Spirituality, and Leisure

"We must learn not to *do* play, but to see play in it all."

David L. Miller
in *Gods and Games*

On a summer evening ice cream outing with a family, the two daughters, ages 7 and 5, were pleasured into silence by the scoops of creamy mocha almond fudge atop their cones. The younger of the two, Lorraine, a sensitive and sensuous child who likes to smell the flowers and stroke kittens' fur, occasionally emitted a low sigh of ecstasy as her tongue brought home yet another marvelous taste.

Then tragedy struck. With her eyes half-closed in dreamy awareness, the sugar cone relaxed in her hand and tilted dangerously. The balls of ice cream teetered from their perch and landed with a splat on the sidewalk. Lorraine's green-blue eyes welled up instantly, and she began to cry in horror and disbelief. The tears made traces down her cheeks, cutting through the ring of mocha almond fudge around her mouth. Her tongue went out instinctively to catch the tears, and in that moment of tasting both the salt of tears and the mocha almond fudge, her eyes flashed the question of human existence: how can life be so sad and so good at the same time?

In *Man at Play* (Herder and Herder, 1967), Hugo Rahner writes that the person who truly "plays" life will never cease to be keenly aware of two things: the first is that existence is joyful because it is secure in God; the second is that it is also a tragic thing, because freedom must always involve peril. Thus, the game of life is both comedy and tragedy for there is no play that has not something profoundly serious at the bottom of it, and no game where there is not some shadow of a possibility that the game may be lost. It is, says Rahner, the synthesis of these two things that

makes the *homo ludens,* the "grave-merry" person, the person
with the gentle sense of humor who laughs despite tears, and finds
in all earthly mirth a sediment of insufficiency. The person who
truly plays must be both joyful and serious at the same time. Much
will go amiss; images of pain will mingle with those of joy, and
both must be affirmed. The ultimate folly, however, would be to
settle for less than the ultimate fact. The folly which God has per-
petrated at Calvary must be given its due. In the play of images
both pleasant and painful, what does it mean to allow such folly
to have the last word?

Rahner rescues from oblivion an allegory of immense worth
as a window into the very real understanding which the Christians
of antiquity possessed of the nature of life as a game requiring both
joy and perseverance. The allegory is built upon a text in Genesis
26:8ff in which we are told how Isaac and his wife Rebecca went
during a time of famine into the land of the Philistines to King
Abimelech. Isaac was afraid that the men there would kill him to
get the beautiful Rebecca if they knew she was his wife. So, in
order to safeguard his life Isaac presented Rebecca as his sister.
But one day King Abimelech looked out his window and saw
Isaac "playing" with Rebecca. The *Good News Bible* simply says
that he "saw Isaac and Rebecca making love." But most other
translations say that Abimelech, "looking out through a window,
saw Isaac playing with Rebecca, his wife." It is thus that King
Abimelech recognizes that they are not brother and sister but a
wedded pair.

Now "Isaac" means "laughter" in Hebrew, while "Rebecca" means "perseverance." According to the allegorical
interpretation, King Abimelech recognizes that laughter and perseverance are wed for life when he sees them enter into "play"
together.

Earnest and Jest are husband and wife, one flesh. In our contemporary Christian life-style of leisure, the challenge is to find

ways of affirming both work and play without idolatrizing either of them. The only way to do that is to place them both in the broader context of life's meaning and purpose, to see them, not as separate and antithetical elements, but as one flesh, as dynamically intertwined responses to a gracious and caring God.

To the Greeks, the art of a truly humane culture appeared in the ability to take life seriously and yet be able to play and, while playing, ever to keep a serious corner in one's mind. Robert Neale says in *In Praise of Play* (Harper and Row, 1969) that the religious person alternates between play for its own sake and work for the sake of other human beings. Without both stresses being acknowledged as complementary, there is only destruction of the individual; with acknowledgement, there is mature adventure, genuine leisure. The most uncommon and yet only viable response to the sacred is grave-merriness, laughter and perseverance lying in love together, tragedy and comedy as a seamless garment. This means that here and now we live with the confidence of a comic nature, judging tragedy as a penultimate word about life and accepting comedy as the ultimate.

Consolidating Our Themes

In this chapter, we will develop a notion of leisure that is strongly anchored in these scriptural themes, totally consistent with holistic living, and that affirms both work and play as one flesh without idolatrizing either of them. The essential content of this understanding of leisure is *freedom*—the sense of freedom one has when one experiences one's uniqueness and worth and feels accepted by and related to the surrounding environment.

But let's retrace our steps for a moment, consolidating the main themes of the first two chapters before taking the next step towards leisure. John Pilch's definition of wellness provides a concise summary of Chapter 1, "The Wellness Revolution."

> Wellness is an ever-expanding experience of pleasurable and purposeful living which you and I, especially as motivated by spiritual values and religious beliefs, create and direct for ourselves in any way we choose.

Pilch then lists five key elements in this concept of wellness:

1 – knowing the purpose and meaning of life;
2 – identifying life's authentic, satisfying, fulfilling human joys and pleasures;
3 – accepting responsibility for freedom or self-determination;
4 – finding an appropriate source of motivation;
5 – accepting the need for change in life, the need for ongoing conversion.

The goal is a positive state of wellness in the whole person, which goes beyond the mere absence of disease. All aspects of a person are involved; one is not emphasized to the detriment of another. We strive for harmony, balance, and integration of the spiritual, emotional, physical and intellectual dimensions of living. Wellness frees us to become what God in God's creative plan and providence both allows and invites. In seeking wellness we will no longer be content with the minimum but will seek to maximize our use of God's gifts.

In Chapter 2, a spirituality for wellness was sketched out after having noted in Chapter 1 that a great deal of the wellness literature today neglects to give equal treatment to the spiritual component of our being. The core notion of Pilch's approach to wellness coalesces harmoniously with the spirituality founded upon the scriptural notion of abundant life. In Chapter 1 we saw that wellness seeks to enhance the quality of our lives. Chapter 2 set forth the spirituality based on the very same quest: more and fuller life. The abundance of life is both our human and our spiritual aim. Hence we are concerned about searching out the possibilities for and the conditions of abundant life.

The correspondence between the themes of Chapter 2 and the five key elements of wellness detailed by Pilch is very close. The first two elements—1) knowing the purpose and meaning of life, and 2) identifying life's fulfilling human joys and pleasures—were given further development in Chapter 2 through an approach to spirituality as the attitudes and convictions which condition and define our vision of the world and our role in it. In this context, we explored the questions of how do we grow, how do we enjoy, and how do we fulfill ourselves.

Pilch's third key element is "accepting responsibility for freedom of self-determination." Among the wellness writers this corresponds to having an aim in life, a purpose; discovering one's responsibility is crucial to discovering one's power. In a spirituality for wellness, we accept that we alone determine what life will mean for us.

This spirituality also addresses Pilch's fourth key element—finding an appropriate source of motivation—by advancing the conviction that the only source of motivation truly capable of summoning a response from every dimension of our being is life itself, more and fuller life, abundant life. If one's spirituality is basically a question of the attitudes and convictions which condition our stance toward the world, spirituality thus has a direct impact on our values, which is to say, on the sources which motivate us in our quest for the fulfillment of our lives. Lest this be seen as merely enlightened selfishness, or warmed-up left-overs from the 70's me-generation fare masquerading as today's new truth, it must be clearly grasped that in the context of the spirituality proposed here, when we speak about the fulfillment of our lives it makes no difference whether we are referring to our lives in the future ("eternity") or here and now. Each of us has only one life to live, if death be seen as a moment wherein life is not ended but merely changed. Hence the continuum which is ultimately life forever has already begun and whether I like it or not I am in eternity.

Consequently, the most compelling motivation for me in living is the quest for an ever-expanding experience of life. To be sure, people will interpret what constitutes an ever-expanding experience of life in extremely varied ways, from Mother Teresa to Hugh Hefner. That is what makes the fifth key element in an understanding of wellness so important: accepting the need for change in life, the need for ongoing conversion.

Chapter 2 sought to address this important concern by setting forth a spirituality according to which spiritual development is woven into human development. Thus, life transitions and change can be seen as moments of conversion and transformation. Spiritual development implies that we confront our self-deceptions and evasions. It means being truthful in our relationships as parents, spouses, teachers, and friends. And if there is one particular area which calls us to the need for ongoing conversion, it is the experience of gratitude.

At the heart of a spirituality for wellness is the picture of the spiritual person as one who is animated by the giftedness of life, especially one's own, and who accepts it with a gratitude profoundly experienced. But, as is the case with any gift that is given, the receiver's thanks only ring sincere when the gift is used in a way that fulfills the purpose of its being given. How do we grow? How do we enjoy? How do we fulfill ourselves? By seizing upon the gift given, our lives, and by living with gratitude, with an intensity and a passion which are unmistakable expressions of our appreciation. Enjoying life to the full is only arrived at through rightful use of the gift. Grateful people are happy people.

These notions of wellness and a spirituality for wellness are valuable in themselves for living. They are set forth here with a particular purpose: to serve as a framework of philosophical and religious principles and convictions for people participating in various forms of leisure activities today. Hopefully, this conceptual framework will help in an approach to those activities in a holistic, wellness-inducing and spiritually growthful way.

The purpose with which I am working with these themes is not as lofty as some might desire. Why develop all these rich notions in relation to certain leisure, sporting activities? The answer is simple. Because a great number of people are investing enormous quantities of time and energy into these activities very possibly without experiencing the full yield from them that they could be. I do not mean to suggest that they are not experiencing *any* satisfaction and fulfillment. Obviously, if such were the case, people would not be engaging in these activities. These reflections are offered in the interest of more and fuller life, the quest for which is very much at the heart of life's meaning. If what I articulate here helps some to view their lives more holistically, to actualize more fully the gifts they have been given, and to live with a greater sense of enthusiasm and gratitude for those gifts, I will consider these efforts worthwhile.

Since my purpose is, then, to treat these themes in relation to leisure activities, yet another strand must be woven into our reflections to this point: what does "leisure" mean?

The Leisure Revolution

In *Work, Play, and Worship in a Leisure-Oriented Society* (Augsburg Publishing House, 1972), Gordon Dahl made a series of analyses of the state of affairs at that time and projections for the future. By Dahl's evaluation, for increasing numbers of Americans and especially for American youth, the god of work, before whom previous generations of Americans have worshiped, is dead. Future generations of Americans will not have the same reverence for work that their ancestors had. While work will still be good and necessary, it will not provide either the personal satisfaction or the social salvation as it once did. People are looking elsewhere for the meaning and purpose of their lives. This sociological shift Dahl terms the "leisure revolution." In the past, much of the motivation for health, education and welfare programs has been based upon the desire to increase economic productivity. In the future, the major stimulus will be the desire to enhance the enjoyment and meaning of human life.

In support of his analysis, Dahl offered an excerpt from a report prepared in 1968 by Merrill Lynch, Pierce, Fenner and Smith, Inc.:

> All indications are that the overall leisure market will keep on growing. We believe that it will reach 250 billion by 1975. What is more, we believe that leisure will be the dynamic element in the domestic economy in the 1970's and that it will even outperform the economy.

A study sponsored by the Canadian Employment and Immigration Commission, Statistics Canada, and the Federal Department of Communications published in June, 1982, indicated that the Merrill Lynch projection was on target for the whole of North America and, if anything, Canadians have fulfilled its prophecy even more so than Americans. The study poked itself into the lives of 2,600 Canadians in 11 cities and 3 rural subdivisions to find out how and where they spend their time and whom they spend it with. It revealed that Canadians spend only 49 hours a week working—this includes work after as well as during office hours, weekend work, etc. That's the lowest number of hours in at least 30 countries, including Finland which boasts of such things. Americans work three to four hours more a week than the Canadian average.

The study also shows that the average Canadian over the age of fourteen devotes seventy-seven hours a week to eating, sleeping, dressing, smoking and drinking, and forty-two hours a week in direct pursuit of leisure.

The economic and educational systems of both American and Canadian societies were developed around the principle of deferred rewards: "Work now, play later," and "Save for a rainy day'' were part of the folk-wisdom on which previous generations on this continent have been reared. Furthermore, there has been a strong tendency in evangelical religion on both sides of the border to equate pleasure with sin. Mass-media advertising, however, has bred a new generation on an addictive pattern of immediate gratification. The vast system of installment credit has made ''buy now and pay later'' possible as a way of life.

Paralleling the economic encouragements toward immediate gratification have been various social movements which have focused attention upon human freedom and fulfillment. The sixties were characterized by the civil rights movement and student protests; the seventies by the human potential movement and the women's liberation movement.

In the 80's the leisure revolution has come into full blossom. Intensive self-help seminars for workaholics have seen their clientele dwindle to that upper-echelon executive ten percent who have to put in extra hours to stay on top. The problem now is, according to many, that people don't work *enough*. Numerous are the politicians and church leaders who appear to be encouraging a return to the virtues of hard work out of a sense of fear that this generation will not be able to channel creatively the energies freed up by the leisure revolution with the resulting end of moral anarchy and social chaos.

At the heart of the question is not just how many hours people work at their jobs, but the fulfillment they derive from what they do. There is no way that spending *more* hours holding a stop sign at a road construction site or dispensing tickets at the local theatre can be equated with a higher life-meaning quotient. The problem has little to do with *quantity* and much to do with *quality* of work and sense of purpose.

Nowhere has this been more evident than in the influx of women into sporting activities that we have witnessed in the 80's. Their participation is fueled by the need for outlets for individual expression and accomplishment, particularly among married women who, either through personal choice or for raising children, remain at home. The need for individual expression or accomplishment may have been met up to marriage through higher education or through work, but often goes unfulfilled in the years following marriage. There is a need for an activity, solitary or shared with others, whose credit for mastery will be uncontestably one's own, and in which one can find one's own worth and value reflected. In this context, training for and running a marathon or winning a doubles tennis tournament can be a deeply symbolic personal statement.

While some applications of this need for personal expression and accomplishment have been positive, other applications have only served to underline fears that energies freed up by the leisure revolution will be narcissistically turned back upon ourselves.

Time magazine's cover story (August 30, 1982) "The New Ideal of Beauty" reported that more than half of all American women—more than half, even, of all U.S. married mothers—are in the labor force. There a woman must collaborate and compete with men, as other men do, as a peer. She is dressing and shaping her body to fit the new fashion of equality. Medicine has made her more aware of how her body works. The fitness phenomenon has proved she has the capacity to make it work. Her new sense of self-assurance has convinced her that strength—of the body, mind and will—is beautiful. Thus, the look of the eighties: a firm body, healthy hair and skin, and a look of serene determination in the eyes.

But some of those interviewed reflected ambivalence and fear around this development. "Women are in danger of turning in on themselves, becoming emotionally muscle-bound" opined one television producer. "We've entered an age of mental and physical narcissism. Originally, man built a strong body to do work. Now women are building their bodies just to look good. Is that enough? Does beauty stop at the skin-line? This kind of woman will be sitting alone, in an empty room, with her perfect body.'' Paul Corkery, a Los Angeles novelist, agrees, adding that the strong woman is chasing form without the function: ''It's as if they're all in training for the Olympics. They're all muscled up with nowhere to go.''

If both women *and* men are to transcend the enlightened narcissism preached by magazines like *Fit* and *New Body*, they will have to learn to exercise for both the inside and the outside. It is precisely toward that process of integration that this book seeks to make some small contribution.

The leisure *revolution* is not too strong a term to use when one considers its impact: new possibilities and problems, new roles and relationships, new values and lifestyles, new hopes and fears. The most perceptive observers of contemporary North American culture do not hesitate to write about a new consciousness, a new mentality, and a new reformation. They not only speak of changes which are occurring in society, but, what is even more significant, changes which are occurring within hearts and minds. Our work, our play and our worship are all being reshaped. Our sense of who we are and what we are doing with life is exposed and our ways of relating to each other are being transformed. It would be naive to face these trends with unqualified enthusiasm, but in general they can be affirmed and celebrated since they represent new surges of human freedom and fulfillment.

The only way out is the way through, and the best way through is the way of harmony, integration and balance. An understanding of leisure that is holistic will contribute to genuine wellness and will not result in moral deterioration and social chaos.

The Work-Ethic

So according to some, we work too much and do not have enough time for leisure pursuits; and for others, we do not work enough and the leisure revolution is a further threat to the moral fibre of society. Obviously what is needed is a notion of leisure that recognizes the value of both work and play but which can find realization in either.

The essential component in such a notion of leisure is *freedom*—an inner, spiritual sense of freedom present in both purposeful work and frivolous play. This quality of freedom-in-one's-spirit penetrates both unstructured time and routine. It is a question of the inner attitude, the sense and style with which both are approached.

Two forces have militated against this understanding of leisure. The first is the puritan work-ethic. The second is the popular notion of leisure as rest, reward from work, free time. We will briefly examine each, identify their shortcomings, and set forth an understanding of leisure that is both scriptural and holistic.

The work-ethic says first of all that a person's work, i.e. one's job, one's occupation, one's profession or whatever one does that pays off in terms of money or its equivalent, is the most important aspect of one's life and takes precedence over all other aspects. Secondly, it says that each one will be rewarded for his or her work, but one must not seek to enjoy that reward until one's work is finished. The work-ethic essentially consists of these two notions: primacy of work and deferred reward.

Max Weber pointed out in his classic essay *The Protestant Ethic and the Spirit of Capitalism* that there is no biblical basis for the so-called Protestant ethic from which the modern work-ethic has evolved. In the creation story, work appears rather as a sign of demotion and banishment, certainly not the mark of nobility or the source of our hope. While the biblical peoples were hard-working, nowhere in Scripture is worldly work exalted as the primary aspect of life or presented as a basis for future rewards. The Israelites were repeatedly reminded that it was not by their human achievements but by their trust in God's promises that their destiny would be fulfilled. Correspondingly, their year was organized around Holy Day periods during which regular work was strictly forbidden. As for Jesus, he not only left his job as a carpenter, but called countless others away from theirs as well, offering frequent warnings to those preoccupied with worldly work and the pursuit of wealth and power: "It will be as difficult for a wealthy person to enter the kingdom of heaven as for a camel to pass through the eye of a needle."

In early Christianity, the monastics gave the first fruits of their day to prayer. Work was something they did in their free time. However, their eagerness to prepare for the kingdom of God fostered a certain disdain for the things of this world which, in turn, resulted in a splitting of human affairs into sacred and secular categories. There were those who took vows of exclusive dedication to "spiritual works" in contrast to those who continued to work at the ordinary tasks of life. The notion of "vocation" narrowed to include only those consecrated to offer special "spiritual works" to God like prayer, meditation, and fasting.

Martin Luther attacked the medieval Church's system of spiritual works as being unfaithful to Scripture. He argued that neither spiritual nor secular work contributes to salvation; only the work of Christ merits salvation. "By the free gift of God's grace all are put right with him through Christ Jesus who sets them free" (Romans 3:24). Luther repudiated the narrow notion of vocation and countered with an integration of two separate biblical concepts: the call to salvation by accepting God's free gift in Jesus Christ, and the admonition to remain steadfast in one's present responsibilities until the return of Christ (Romans 13:12).

Calvin taught that we are called neither to spiritual works nor to quiet acceptance of God's justifying grace, but to actively glorify God in work. Viewing themselves as the stewards of God's creation, Calvinists sought to shore up the functioning of nature with their own efforts. The most militant of them became known as Puritans and each one had his own special role, or "calling" through which he glorified God in a direct and personal way.

Though it was a misapplication of Calvin's teaching, the Puritan evolution of his teaching was such that if one was prospering in one's calling, it was discerned that one was enjoying the blessing of God which, of course, suggested that one was among the elect.

> For the Puritans, therefore, secular work took on profound spiritual significance. They knew that they could not earn salvation by their work, but they had no other basis upon which to assess their spiritual condition nor any other means of expressing their religious devotion. It became a matter of religious necessity that every aspect of their lives, as well as every aspect of their social and natural environment, be brought under the discipline of rational control and development. While Catholics, Lutherans, and the evangelical sects could experience an assurance of salvation through occasional flourishes of piety, the faithful Puritan was subject to a lifetime of systematic self-improvement and a desperate quest for worldly success lest his earthly life show the symptoms of being bound for hell. This dedication to self-improvement and success became the Puritan's ethic, or as Weber called it, the Protestant ethic. (Dahl, pp. 47–48)

While popular opinion and Dahl's analysis have relegated the Puritan ethic to our national socio-cultural museum, there is data to suggest that it is still alive and kicking out in the streets. In 1982, United Media Enterprises undertook a study of Americans' use of leisure time entitled "Where Does the Time Go?" The survey on leisure was based on telephone interviews with more than one thousand randomly selected people in all fifty states. The pollsters turned up surprisingly traditional attitudes. Most respondents said leisure had to be earned with work. Seven out of ten said hardly any of their free time is wasted and six out of ten said excess time is best spent when it focuses on goals. Says social scientist John Pollock who supervised the study: "Our flinty Puritan heritage has its hooks in the present."

There seems little question that we still find it difficult to give ourselves permission to use time in a Sabbath rhythm as did the Israelites. The notion of resting in God is embedded in every great religious tradition. Sabbath time is sensual time: a time for good eating, pleasant candlelight, family singing, subdued talk, and enjoyment of the physical as well as of the spiritual dimensions of our lives. While this tradition is clearly in the Christian way as well, fewer and fewer are the Christians who could say with Eric in "Chariots of Fire": "God made countries; God made kings and the rules by which they govern. His law is that the Sabbath is his, and I for one intend to keep it that way."

It is immensely difficult for us to give ourselves permission to use time for being still, for being silent, for seeking nothing, for "wasting time with God"—and with regularity, not just when our backs are to the wall and we are too worn out to work at keeping control. I can witness to this as a personal truth. One of the ways that the fifth key element of wellness (accepting the need for change in life, the need for ongoing conversion) incarnates itself in my life is learning how not to *do* play, but to see play in it all.

I suspect that I will be experiencing conversion in this area across the whole of my life. The inherent worthwhileness of ministry, the desire to serve others, to care compassionately for the Church and for society, makes it all the more difficult to claim non-productive time. The result is that slowly and subtly one can be drawn into a belief system that espouses (often in disguised ways) justification by works. The "common democratic religion" that Alexis de Tocqueville discerned in his visit to America wears many guises and manifests itself in many subtle forms: "It is, in short, a religion characterized by a belief in the ultimate perfectibility of man and his society and by a devotion to work as the means of achieving that perfection."

Who among us has not at one time or another experienced the syndrome where moments of relaxation become rare or nonexistent? We feel rushed and pushed. If there is something to be done we cannot rest until it is finished. When one project is over there is always another to be tackled. The moments when we feel we can stop are few and far between. Martin C. Helldorfer, in his book *The Work Trap* (Affirmation Books, 1983), touches a nerve when he asks:

> Why do we work so much? Why do we never seem to have time to be with others? Why do we not have time to relax or even play? We say we work incessantly because we have to . . . because we like to . . . because we are expected to . . . because we are devoted . . . because there doesn't seem to be anyone else to do it . . . because. . . . The reasons that we give to explain our way of living are often attempts to justify ourselves. (p. 15)

Helldorfer characterizes one who is work-fixated as "being always and everywhere project-oriented." When this occurs and to the degree that it occurs, one sees the world in terms of something to be changed, and one divides it into what is useful and not-so-useful, holding everything and everyone slightly apart from oneself in order to move them according to one's purpose.

While there is nothing subtle about overwork (we usually know it when we have crossed over the line), the problem lies in feeling that we cannot stop: "There is still so much unfinished that needs to be done that I really must stay with it."

We may find ourselves enmeshed in this situation precisely because we are competent. When something needs to be done it is not the incompetent that people turn to. The kind of person sought is the one who immediately recognizes what needs to be done and who can do it better and more efficiently than many others. It is not long, asserts Helldorfer, before the talented person both sees and is asked to do more than is humanly possible:

> But competency alone is not the culprit. It is when competency exists side by side with unfulfilled needs that problems

arise. If we have unusually strong needs to please others, to appear generous or self-sacrificing or if we are pushed to excel or be in charge, or to have power, and if at the same time we are highly talented, we are particularly vulnerable to overwork. There is almost no way to avoid it. We want to be helpful and we can do many things well. The difficulty is that it is not long before we lose our vibrancy in the midst of too much to do. Called "burn-out" this problem exists among many professionals. (p. 31)

Dahl describes three other contemporary ailments which all spring from the conception that the meaning and value of leisure comes from its relationship to work: 1) *work addiction;* 2) *the exodus complex* (the compulsive pursuit of freedom from everyday routine, the compulsive need to keep moving, to be always going somewhere—anywhere—to get away from it all); and 3) *justifiable suicide* (or, in other words, "I earned it, and I'm going to enjoy it even if it kills me"—and often it does!). Those who suffer from these neuroses never seem to experience any real leisure, but simply burn themselves out trying to work harder and play harder. "Ours is the only society in the history of civilization," says Dahl, "that offers its people the choice of working themselves to death or consuming themselves to death, or both."

We Want More From Life Than Work Can Offer

The two great hungers in American society today, for spiritual meaning and for physical fitness, even while for many people running parallel to one another without intersecting, testify to the desperate search for a scheme of meanings and values that will bring quality and satisfaction into our lives. Work may have brought us comfort, security and status, but we want more from life than what work can offer. Many college students already have a clear sense today even before their graduation that while they want to work, they do not wish to make work the center of their lives. Their own experience as a leisure class, their exposure to the media, and often their own parents' hurried, worried, and work-oriented lifestyles have served to convince them that the way to the good life will be the one that balances work with other pursuits.

In his book *Megatrends* (Warner Books, 1983), John Naisbitt offers encouragement and gives additional reasons why the seeking of such a balance makes a lot of sense. The restructuring of society in North America from an industrial to an information-oriented society will be as profound as the shift from an agricultural society to an industrial one, but with a difference. While the latter took a century, the former is only taking about two decades. Naisbitt believes that individuals are not helpless in shaping the development and use of computer technology and that the Church with its accumulated wisdom can play a very helpful supporting role in these explorations.

We live in "the parenthesis," as Naisbitt calls it, between two ages, and we need to manage this gap and make it a fruitful time. The Church, while helping people to recognize their past as vital and integral to their development, can direct them to a new lifestyle, a new worldview, a new involvement in life. Because of the basic ingredients of technology, men and women will be challenged to balance the material with the spiritual, the "high tech" with the "high touch."

To the question "How?", what we have already said on the subjects of wellness and spirituality provides the answer. Through a spirituality for wellness, contemporary Christians will develop a consciousness of the abundance of alternatives for making their lives meaningful. Because both the notions of wellness and spirituality relate to the quest for more and fuller life (not understood as enlightened egocentrism but as bearing the responsibility of free, moral agents in the world), wellness and its spirituality challenge us to transform our social systems in order to enable all human beings to enjoy a full share of economic, social, and spiritual *freedom.*

Leisure or freedom is essentially a spiritual experience, rather than an economic or social condition, but economic and social trends have both nurtured and been nurtured by the spiritual experience of leisure. The chief characteristic of leisure in our civilization must be its integrative and harmonizing function.

How we handle this leisure, this freedom, and according to what values, will determine the direction of both our religious tradition and the civilization it has nurtured. And it is the Gospel itself—not merely the fascinating, complex social changes which we are witnessing—that is calling and challenging us to new consciousness and a new sharing of our freedom.

Shortcomings of Popular Notions about Leisure

Dahl makes a frontal attack on the three most popular notions about leisure to be found in our society. Leisure is not free time. Leisure is not rest or reward from work. Leisure is not simply constructive entertainment or distraction.

1. Leisure is not free time

To begin with, the whole notion of free time is theologically unfounded. For a Christian, all of one's time is free—life has been given and redeemed by God apart from any work on one's own part. Life is a gift, given freely and intended to be received and enjoyed by people when they are at work as well as when they are at play. On the other hand, *none* of a Christian's time is free time in the sense that one is free to do anything that one pleases with it. We are to offer our *lives* as a "living sacrifice" to God, whether working or playing. In his writings about Christian freedom, Luther described a Christian as one who always lives in both total freedom and total responsibility.

In spite of this present time being called the Age of Leisure, the simple fact is that many feel that they simply have no such thing as free time. Where does that leave them as far as leisure is concerned? Some experience their greatest freedom when they are working and others are anything but free when they are cut off from their work. Of those people in North American society today who do have an abundance of free time, perhaps the greater part of them are those who in some sense have been removed from active participation (the hospitalized, imprisoned, the involuntarily disemployed or retired); one could hardly call their situation free and certainly not consider it to be leisure. Leisure, then, cannot be simply made to equal free time.

2. Leisure is not rest or reward from work

In both the religious and secular views of the world which have dominated the development of thought in North America, the human person was conceived as a worker whose primary role was to labor at his particular place in the system. Most of our economic and educational systems have been built upon this notion.

The problem with the rationalist concept of *homo faber* (the human person as worker) is that it obscured *homo ludens* (the human person as player). For the Puritans and rationalists, any form of idleness was suspect unless it could be justified in terms of work, either as purifying the mind for more dedicated and disciplined service, or resourcing the body for more of the same. And yet all those who have studied the play element in culture and who are repeatedly cited in this context (Johan Huizinga, Hugo Rahner, Peter Berger, Robert Neale, David Miller, and Jurgen Moltmann) are of one accord that play is connected with no material interest and is valuable for its own sake. Unless there is meaning and value in the experience itself, apart from any significance in relationship to work, it will not have the freedom nor the authentic self-expression which makes it truly leisure, and appreciation of the experience as such will be diminished.

3. Leisure is not simply constructive entertainment or distraction

This notion is particularly prevalent among those who invest nearly all of their energy and interest in their work and who, therefore, have little to bring or give to a genuine leisure experience. In this case, the quest for leisure is reduced to simple entertainment, distraction, or escape. Relaxation is sought in the form of escape from pressures through sleep, drink, drugs, or indiscriminate watching of television. The oscillation then is not between activity and rest, but between achievement and escape.

While entertainment can be very enjoyable and refreshing, few people can live on entertainment alone or find sufficient *freedom* in a routine of work and distraction.

What Leisure Is

Dahl points us in the direction of classical antiquity to uncover the original meaning of leisure as it appears in the writings of Greek and Roman philosophers and poets. In every instance, leisure is understood and valued as a creative and liberating experience whose root meaning is *freedom*. Not free time, or freedom from work, or political freedom, or the so-called freedom of no commitments in relationships. In Dahl's words:

> Leisure is rather that sense of freedom which is realized when a person experiences more fully both his uniqueness and worth as an individual and his acceptance and relationship as part of the world around him. A person finds leisure when he discovers who he is, what he can do with his life, and what an abundance of happy circumstances and relationships in which his life is cast. A Christian experiences leisure when he comes into full awareness of the freedom he has in Christ, the freedom from fear and guilt because of sin but, even more important, the freedom to be and become a new creation after Christ's own splendid example. (pp. 70–71)

Note the profound resonance here with our already-developed notions of wellness and spirituality:

• Leisure is experienced when one realizes and lives more fully both one's uniqueness and worth as an individual	Wellness is an ever-expanding experience of life
• Leisure is experienced when one discovers who one is, what one can do with one's life, and responds to the circumstances and relationships in which one's life is cast	Spirituality is basically a question of the attitudes and convictions which condition our stance toward the world and our response to it

Leisure, then, according to this understanding of it, is closely allied to scriptural themes and to a holistic approach to living.

To his brief definition of leisure, Dahl adds a few descriptive statements toward constructing a concept of leisure which will adequately convey its contemporary meaning:

1. **Leisure is essentially spiritual, rather than economic or social in character.**

The economic and social freedoms which we have gained in recent decades will mean little if we merely exchange them for new, modern forms of bondage, e.g., to our technology. Leisure is the very freedom that allows and enables us to occasionally transcend the dimensions of economic and social necessity and participate in higher realities. At the same time as it transcends our economic circumstances and social arrangements, it must also penetrate them, touching both our own soul and that of our culture. First and foremost, leisure must affect our spirits, causing them to soar and enabling our humanity to find larger expression. This kind of leisure goes far beyond our schedules and the particles of time parcelled out therein, and is more properly described as a partaking of eternity.

2. Leisure is a quality or style of life, rather than fragments of a lifetime.

On this point, Dahl's words strike me as so critical that I do not wish to risk detracting anything from them by means of summary:

> Conceived as quality of life rather than as quantities of time, leisure requires no arbitrary distinctions between work and play, between that which is important and necessary and that which is unimportant or optional. Leisure can be experienced during times of work as well as times of play, in activity which is crucial as well as that which is frivolous. It will often mean freedom from work, at least freedom from the routines and requirements of work, but it need not be (and, indeed, should not be) juxtaposed against work as if they were experiences which were somehow incompatible. Work and play will shape the schedule of people's lives, but leisure provides the sense and style with which they go about it all . . . enabling them to discover the presence of grace and peace in their daily walk. (pp. 73–74)

At first glance, it appears that the leisure revolution has its primary value in that it offers us alternatives to work. But upon further discernment, it is clear that its real significance is in liberating us from achievement- and production-oriented values, from the meritorious meanings which have provided the cadence for society's marching gait up to this point. "Leisurely" is a word that accurately describes the style of life of a people who live theologically by grace through faith in Christ, and sociologically in the midst of an unprecedented abundance of created goods and opportunities for the enlargement of the human spirit.

3. Leisure is a synthesizing factor in our "component" civilization.

The rationalization of human experience which began with the Renaissance and Reformation and which has provided the framework for modern civilization has subjected to critical analysis not only every aspect of our universe but humanity itself, reducing every aspect of our experience to various component parts. Dahl suggests that most middle class North Americans have these component parts confused: "We worship our work, we work at our play, and we play at our worship." We are therefore missing much of the joy which is available to us by virtue of our freedom as Christians and our abundance as North Americans. Many today are experiencing these elements as competing and conflicting interests. Leisure as a synthesizing factor in our component civilization means the reality in which we live—our work, our commitments, our relationships—is to be seen as a single whole, a whole by means of which God interacts with us, inviting us to more and fuller life. When leisure is looked at in the particular perspective traced out in these pages,

> we do not speak of the fact that we may spend too much time in an office, kitchen, or workshop. Neither do we refer to the need for more leisure time or to the need to find interesting leisure-time activities. We do not praise the value of *being* at the expense of the value of *doing,* or vice versa. What we are speaking about is leisure as a way of living and as a component of all involvement whether the activity is a job, game, prayer, or sleep. If there is an observation that we wish to accent, it is this: that despite all our activity, the reality seems to be that we are under- rather than over-involved. Our busyness reflects a condition of being scattered. . . . We need to be slowed by involvement. (Martin Helldorfer, *The Work Trap,* p. 49)

To describe what he means by "we need to be slowed by involvement," Helldorfer gives the example of how people move leisurely through museums. They become involved. The condition for their becoming involved is that they have enough distance to notice but not so much as to be detached. Living in the spirit of leisure described here is similar: if we stand too far from or too close to life we risk not noticing what is before us. Rushing through each day in harried fashion would be like running through a museum while never noticing what was there. There would never be time for our senses to catch or be caught by wonderment. In other words, we would be uninvolved. In this sense, leisure is not something which must first be achieved or else wrested from our duties in the work place, but it is itself a characteristic of *involvement* in whatever we are doing. Hence, leisurely living has more to do with facilitating genuine involvement than with willful efforts to slow down. If we become involved, the slowing-down process will take place automatically.

Thus, Helldorfer concludes, "the issue surrounding work, work-fixation, and leisure is not that of being too involved. Neither is it a question of working too little. Rather what is at issue is the base from which we are involved" (p. 59).

We Were Created for a Life of Leisure

Institutional Christianity has at different times in history worked itself into the corner of thinking it must persevere simply as an agent to prepare people for heaven. Interpreting pilgrimage in terms of an ultimate goal, eternal life, it missed the thrust of Jesus' own teaching that *eternal life is a quality of the pilgrimage itself:* "Eternal life is this: to know you, the only true God, and Jesus Christ whom you have sent" (John 17:5). If eternal life is essentially knowing God, how wonderfully enjoyable God must be!

Perhaps we have made God too useful to be very enjoyable. When God becomes useful, e.g. helping us out of messes, rewarding our obedience with health and wealth and happiness, religion becomes a utilitarian exchange—the solemn business of giving God the service God requires and asking that God do the same for us. We then relate to God the same way that we relate to one another: we demand of another that she prove herself, earn her way, show herself useful. The other, like God, is justified by works.

Joseph McLelland in *The Clown and the Crocodile* (John Knox, 1970) notes that Marx and Freud have *served* the Gospel by giving clear warnings about this kind of false, utilitarian religion. Christians tend to miss the point, thinking they have to choose between seeking a new society on earth and awaiting one in heaven.

But if persons are to be enjoyed more than used, could we not love God for God's own sake, or because this is the finest and most ennobling thing we can do?

Do we dare hold that there is no other reward for loving God besides the experience itself? Do we dare hold that our living in love of God *is* essentially our salvation? Love unites, and so brings us into union with God and with all else in God.

To approach it any other way than this is to make of God an instrument for the attainment of something: God is for salvation, God is for supernatural life, or God is for heaven. To speak thus is to dishonor a relationship of love with the cheap language of buying and selling. As anyone who has ever loved knows, we cannot use a loving relationship with another *for* anything. Neither can we love another *for* anything. We love, rather, because the relationship of loving is the most creative, the most life-enhancing, the most self-enlivening of all possible relationships. And most of all, we love because we cannot resist the sheer beauty and loveliness and goodness of the Other.

Living in this relationship of love provides a life of leisure. Leisure conceived as quality of life rather than quantity of free time—a quality which can be experienced during times of work and times of play. A quality which provides the sense and style with which one goes about either work or play when one is *involved* in it. When this is the case, Earnest and Jest are husband and wife, one flesh. Both work and play are affirmed by placing both in the broader context of life's meaning and purpose and seeing them as dynamically intertwined responses to a gracious and caring God. Leisure is a quality that emanates from the experience of being loved and freely responding in love across every aspect of our living. Believe it or not, we were truly created for a life of leisure!

Chapter 4

A Leisurely, Holistic Approach to Sports

When he prepared the heavens, I was present . . . when he compassed the sea within bounds, and set a law to the waters that they should not pass their limits; when he balanced the foundations of the earth, I was with him forming all things, and was delighted every day, playing before him at all times, playing in the world, and my delights were to be with the human race.

Wisdom 8:27–30

In his classic work *Homo Ludens, A Study of the Play Element in Culture* (Beacon Press, Boston, 1950), Johan Huizinga provides a learned survey for the development of the notion of sport. His research indicates that the medieval Christian ideal left little room for the organized practice of sport and the cultivation of bodily exercise, except insofar as the latter contributed to "gentle education." Similarly, the Renaissance affords fairly numerous examples of body-training cultivated for the sake of perfection, but only on the part of individuals, never groups or classes. If anything, the emphasis laid by the humanists on learning and erudition tended to perpetuate the old under-estimation of the body, as did the moral zeal and severe intellectuality of the Reformation and Counter-Reformation. The recognition of games and bodily exercises as important cultural values was withheld right up to the end of the eighteenth century.

Ever since the last quarter of the nineteenth century, games, in the guise of sport, have been taken more and more seriously. The rules became increasingly strict and elaborate. Records were established at a faster rate than anyone ever thought possible. But, with the increasing systematization of sport, something of the pure play quality was inevitably lost. The spirit of the professional is no longer the true play-spirit; it is lacking in spontaneity, in carelessness. The transformation of sport into a commercial business pushed it further and further away from the play-sphere proper to it.

By contrast, the great competitions in ancient cultures had always formed part of the sacred festivals and were indispensable as health and happiness-bringing activities. This ritual tie, according to Huizinga, has now been completely severed:

> Sport has become profane, 'unholy' in every way; it has no organic connection whatever with the structure of society, least of all when prescribed by the government. The ability of modern social techniques to stage mass demonstrations with the maximum of outward show in the field of athletics does not alter the fact that neither the olympiads nor the organized sports of American universities nor the loudly trumpeted international contests have, in the smallest degree, raised sport to the level of a culture-creating activity. However important it may be for the players or spectators, it remains sterile. The old play-factor has undergone almost complete atrophy. (pp. 197–198)

By way of emphasizing the fatal shift toward over-seriousness, Huizinga points out that it has also infected the non-athletic games such as chess and some card games where calculation is everything. In short, the history of modern sport shows us play stiffening into seriousness while still being called play. Many examples could be given to support these assertions today, from little league baseball to bantam hockey to college football. Still, in the 35 years since Huizinga wrote, other voices have been raised and other movements founded for the preservation or restoration of the play-quality in sports.

A little booklet of pastoral reflections was published on the occasion of the 1976 Olympics in Montreal and entitled *A Christian View of Sports*. "The evangelization of the sports world is in urgent and pressing need of theological reflection," it declares, "and an interpretation and an expression of the Christian message as it applies to sporting activity . . ." (#20).

If the message is grace, then theology's medium must be graceful. If the message is spirit, then the body's flesh must be inspirited. David Miller in *Gods and Games* (World Publishing

Company, 1970) shows how any theological approach to sport or play must incarnate its content. His quest for the meaning of play is itself conceived as a game and is playfully shaped:

> A theology of play might help. But it would not be theo*logy*. It might be more like . . . *theography:* writing about the gods, like geography, mapping where the gods go, where the spirit is.
>
> A theology of play as theography would view things differently. The old things would seem new.
>
> It would think of resting on the first day of the week rather than the seventh. Leisure, contemplation, holiday, and play do not come at the end of work; they are the bases of all life.
>
> Theography would prefer Mary to Martha, the former being one who sees the practicality of the impractical, the value of playing around.
>
> It would see with Jacob Boehme that Adam fell from paradise when his 'play became serious business.'
>
> It would understand Sri Ramakrishna's answer to the problem of theodicy. 'Why, God being good, is there evil in the world?' 'To thicken the plot.''
>
> Theography of play would likely think that bearing witness sounds burdensome and plodding, and would therefore hope to bare witness.
>
> And of course it would likely lead from theography to theo-graffiti: a theology of the everyday, seeing the spirit of life in all life. (p. 176)

Faith must penetrate all aspects of the human condition, including its physical aspects. The more human our spirit becomes the more it will identify itself with our body; and divine grace, to be truly human, must, like the Word of God, become flesh and dwell among us so that we may exclaim together with St. John: ''We have heard it, and we have seen it with our eyes; yes we have seen it, and our eyes have touched it. When this life became visible, we saw it. . . . What we have seen and heard we announce to you also so that . . . your joy may be complete'' (John 1:1–4).

It was in this vein that on November 24, 1984, John Paul II spoke to European Olympic athletes who had participated in the Los Angeles Games:

> Your profession as athletes offers you, among other things, also the opportunity to improve your own personal spiritual state. Called as you are frequently to engage in your competitions in the midst of nature, amid the marvels of the mountains, seas, fields and slopes, you are in the best position to perceive the value of simple and immediate things, the call to goodness, the dissatisfaction with one's insufficiency, and to meditate on the authentic values that are at the basis of human life.
>
> Discipline too, necessary for engaging in athletic performances, can be considered a prerequisite for spiritual elevation . . . and for a training of the spirit through the exercise of the virtues of prudence, justice, fortitude and temperance as well as the virtues of faith, hope and charity.
>
> Beloved young athletes, if you do all this you will be not only excellent athletes but also good Christians and exemplary citizens who can witness to a certain lifestyle both in the sporting arenas and in the environments, even more demanding, of your family and society.

The committed Christian is not called to live out and spread his or her faith over and above his or her sporting activity, but rather to do so within its framework. Further, the sports environment, enlightened by faith and sustained by hope, becomes one's spiritual environment, to the point that, in one's sporting pursuits, one manifests one's Christian commitment at the same time and through the same acts.

It goes without saying that sportspersons may pursue several objectives at the same time, and these objectives need not be mutually exclusive because they are located at different levels of one's consciousness. The theological motivation, however, drawing its vision from the spirituality for wellness articulated in Chapter 2, cuts across these various layers, penetrating, absorbing, and drawing them into its movement toward God.

If the glory of God is the human person fully alive, as Irenaeus of Lyon so beautifully put it, then the Christian, amid the welling-up of all the energies of his being, will be more sensitive still to the bodily splendor that results from a development of his physical resources through the practice of sport. St. Paul wrote to the Corinthians that they should glorify God in their bodies.

Like any other cultural activity, sport can be infused with values rich in meaning, making sporting activities expressive of abundant life lived in grateful freedom—values, in other words, of wellness, spirituality, and leisure.

Sports as a Medium for More and Fuller Life

Everywhere one looks today, people are jogging, biking, hiking, swimming, playing tennis, skiing, doing yoga. It seems as if North America has gone crazy rediscovering the joys of the body. The Miller Lite Report on American Attitudes Toward Sport (*New York Times,* March 20, 1983) reveals that only 3.7 percent of the American population 14 years and older is virtually uninvolved in sports, and that 44 percent of the country participates *daily* in some kind of athletic activity.

Teachers, coaches, and a new spate of athletic magazines praise the virtues of sports and their effects on the learning process and the harmonious development of personality:

- sport channels, increases and regulates the body's physical energies;

- sport sets in motion the individual's mental faculties of attention, observation, analysis, order, judgment, and evaluation;

- sport contributes to the building of character: self-awareness and self-control, knowledge of one's own limitations, endurance, perseverance in effort, and determination to succeed;

- sport contributes to a kind of social education: the "with-against" dynamic of sporting competition involves the person in active interpersonal relationships which raise questions of mutual assistance, conscience, justice, respect for the other, submission to the rules, cooperation, sharing, and camaraderie among people who share the experience.

Continued John Paul to the European athletes:

These are virtues that harmonize well with the Christian spirit because they demand a capacity for self-control, self-denial, sacrifice and humility, and therefore an attitude of gratefulness to God, who is the giver of every good and therefore also the giver of the necessary physical and intellectual talents. Sports are not merely the exercise of muscles, but it is the school of moral values and of training in courage, in perseverance, and in overcoming laziness and carelessness. There is no doubt that these values are of greatest interest for the formation of a personality which considers sports not an end in itself but as a means to total and harmonious physical, moral and social development.

Anyone who has participated in team sports will be able to validate any number of these assertions in one's own experience. An identifiable turning point in my transition from adolescence to adulthood took place on the football field in the final game of my senior year. We were desperately protecting a fragile 13–7 lead with two and a half minutes remaining on the clock. Our number 1 ranking in the state was on the line, as well as the desire of us seniors to make our last game a winning effort. The ball was in our possession on our own 35 yard line; it was fourth down and two yards to go for the first down which would in all likelihood enable us to run out the clock. But could we be sure of making that first down? Failure to do so would turn the ball over to our opponents deep in our own territory with plenty of time left for them to score.

Our coach signaled for time-out and as offensive captain I jogged over to the sidelines to receive his judgment. The scenario was a familiar one. A hundred times that season I had run to the sidelines to get his decision and bring it back out to the team for execution.

This time, however, it was different. He stood in silence for several moments, his eyes flitting back and forth between the scoreboard clock and our field position. In his tense expression it was clear: he wanted this state championship as much as we did. When he spoke, I felt myself tighten with surprise.

"What do you think we should do?" he said. He had never asked that before, and I realized I had come, not to discuss and think through the situation together, but to receive *his* answer. This time he was waiting for *my* answer. All of a sudden I felt the weight of the decision on my shoulders. That moment was a rite of passage.

When I ran back out onto the field, feeling the responsibility for my teammates' hopes as well as my own, it was my decision I brought back to the huddle. "O.K. Go with it," the coach had said when I told him that their linemen had been consistently quicker than ours all night and that I thought a punt was the best way to go.

They took the punt and drove back down the field. With ten seconds remaining on the clock, they had the ball on our 6 yard line. The gun went off as their last-ditch pass was batted up into the air in the end-zone and came down into the hands of our line-backer. Pandemonium reigned! The decision had worked . . . by the slightest of margins.

From that night on, decisions came easier for me. Not only decisions of small import, but decisions that were to significantly affect my life: where I would go to college, what career pattern I would follow, etc. I am convinced that the metamorphosis of my character development benefited largely from my experiences in sports and the relationships that sports occasioned for me.

Not too long ago I spent the better part of a year in France, Switzerland, and Italy. I was mightily impressed with the long hours the high school students in those countries spent at school and over the books in the evening doing homework. In discussing with several students about their curriculum, it became apparent to me in short order that students in some of the European countries finish their secondary schooling with an amount of information in their heads which far outstrips that absorbed by even the better North American students in the same period of study. But even before I learned that these same European students had no opportunity as part of their years in school to participate in co-curricular activities such as drama, band, and athletic teams, I had already observed a lesser-degree of social maturity, of easeful interaction between the sexes, and of the ability to function gracefully under pressure.

When the students whom I met informed me that any sporting activities they engage in are on their own time, generally on weekends, only then did I understand what I had previously observed. The truth presented to me by my own experience is that, while academic information was certainly gleaned in the classroom, my psycho-socio-sexual development and integration took place largely in the locker room, on the athletic field, and on the dance floor after the game. My impression was while the average 17 year old European student carried twice as much information, he or she was not as well-rounded as the typical North American counterpart, at least at that particular stage of growth and development.

More and more the athletic revolution in North America has been looked at in terms of its potential for human growth. For example, the American Alliance for Health, Physical Education, and Recreation has been a major force in developing the "New Physical Education." The goal of the new PE is participation for all. Training starts in the lower grades, with body movements and success-oriented activities designed to help children develop a positive sense of their bodies—the key factor in their eventual self-images. The upper grades are introduced to "lifetime sports," i.e., sports they can participate in for the rest of their lives like sailing, tennis, backpacking, or skiing.

Another development has been what is called the "inner game" approach. Probably the best known proponent of the inner approach is Tim Gallway, author of *Inner Game of Tennis* and *Inner Skiing*. The inner game approach, which we shall give more attention to later, is based on the thesis that we have the ability to perform at a much higher level than we normally do. The insights we gain by means of the inner game approach can help us to improve the quality of our lives—as well as to help us develop a formidable backhand or a graceful parallel turn.

Those "breakthrough moments," when, for no apparent reason, everything seems to click and we perform better than we ever thought possible, give us glimpses of the potentials that exist within us. Bob Kriegel has noted in an article entitled "A Sport for Everybody" (*Holistic Life Handbook,* And/Or Press, 1978, p. 356) that through skiing, rock climbing, and white-water rafting, we learn how to deal with and overcome fear and anxiety. Through running, swimming, or biking long distances we develop endurance and will and learn how to deal with boredom. Through golf we can practice intense concentration and subtle control. Team sports can teach us the value of cooperation.

Though there is an unmistakable utilitarian note about these evaluations of the different sports, the personal growth benefits cited are more of the nature of happy side-effects rather than the reasons which motivate participation itself. The new physical education with its stress upon a sport for everyone is returning the play-element to sports, the loss of which was mourned by Johan Huizinga. There is a growing movement to approach game-playing just for the fun, the challenge, the excitement, and the joy of the play itself. This alone is sufficient incentive for participation. In a culture that is so serious and goal-oriented, these activities provide us with the genuine replenishment of the inner spirit which is the heart of true leisure.

Play's ability to construct an enclave within the serious world of everyday life causes sociologist Peter Berger to call it a "signal of the transcendent." He does not use "transcendent" in a technical philosophical sense, but literally: play enables us to transcend the normal everyday world by inserting us into the time structure of the playful universe which has the specific quality of becoming eternity.

> Some little girls are playing hopscotch in the park. They are completely intent on their game, closed to the world outside it, happy in their concentration. Time has stood still for them—or, more accurately, it has been collapsed into the movements of the game. The outside world has, for the duration of the game, ceased to exist. And, by implication (since the little girls may not be very conscious of this), pain and death, which are the law of that world, have also ceased to exist. Even the adult observer of this scene, who is perhaps all too conscious of pain and death, is momentarily drawn into the beatific immunity. (*A Rumor of Angels,* Anchor Books, 1970, page 59.)

It is this curious quality which belongs to all joyful play that explains the liberation and peace such play provides. Joyful play appears to suspend or bracket the reality of our "living toward death." In early childhood this suspension is unconscious because there is as yet no consciousness of death. In later life, play brings about a beatific reiteration of childhood. "When adults play with genuine joy," writes Berger, "they momentarily regain the deathlessness of childhood." Thus play becomes a "signal of the transcendent" because it points beyond itself, beyond our "nature" to the "super-natural."

Play is part of a whole array of means for regenerating one's strength, for making the most of one's yearning for carefree enjoyment. In order for play to be truly restful and relaxing, truly *freeing,* it must remain play. The player must not become a worker. We need to reown the play content of sporting activity as fundamental for a high level of wellness.

Integrating a balance of labor and leisure into our lives gives yield to an inner peace and freedom. Adrian Van Kaam and Susan Muto testify in "Play and the Spiritual Life" that faith in God's care frees one from over-concern about the results of one's work. Knowing that salvation is God's gift, I can "waste time" periodically, closing my eyes to the piles of unfinished work and allowing the solemn call of duty to fade into the distance.

And when I return from play, there is a renewed energy. I am not as tense and anxious as before, not as prone to be impatient. Somewhere amongst the scattered bowling pins, or lying on the bottom of the swimming pool, that deadly serious attitude toward life lies unconscious—knocked out for the count . . . at least for today. I do not always have to be an achiever in life; I can also be a celebrator of what is given.

Play is a time break in a life of service and obligation. My parents regularly take their grandchildren for a couple of days so that my brothers and sister and their spouses can go apart and refresh themselves through golf, canoeing, or at a local lake resort. By making room in our schedule of duties, we follow the way of

Wisdom who was by God's side, "ever at play in his presence, at play everywhere in the world" (Proverbs 8:31).

There is no playfulness possible when I feel weighed down with worry and refuse to waste a minute. It does wonders for my perspective to recall that my Creator is personally concerned with even the likes of sparrows and their needs—how much more, then, of us, who are "much more than many sparrows" (Matthew 6:25–34). If I lose my capacity for play, I lose my capacity for "useless" presence to the Divine, the heart of prayer: presence simply responding to Presence. Contemplation is, at base, no more than this. Instead of filling every minute, then, it might be good to take time off and enjoy all that is.

Quite possibly in the beginning we will need to look at play in terms of its usefulness in re-creating us for the sake of our work. Such an attitude is not to be despised. It represents an important starting point. If we give ourselves over to play enough, it may eventually be experienced as a value in itself.

One contribution of contemporary Christians to society would be the preservation and development of the play elements of sport. Churches should encourage play on all levels as part of their mission of evangelization in contemporary society. If not from the Church, from what quarter can we hope for support in diminishing our idolatrous attachment to work? Allowing the spirit of play to enter into all levels of life is an integral part of the Christian mission to society.

Where modern society moves toward mechanization, sport tends toward personalization. Where modern society breeds individualism, play fosters socialization. Where modern technology makes it easier for us to be passive, play summons us to be active. Sports gather together in solidarity. Team sports, with all their values of communalism, belonging, and collaboration, deserve much larger treatment than they receive in these pages. Most of my own sporting experience prior to graduating from university was within the context of team sports like baseball, basketball, football, hockey, and volleyball. Once out of school, however, the opportunity for team sports is hard to come by.

While I am well aware of the rich source of value-laden reflections that team sports represent, the decision to give priority in the second half of this book to individual sports flowed from the observation that the majority of potential readers have many more opportunities to engage in individual rather than team activities. Team sports, however, best typify the ways in which play counter-balances some of the individualistic, self-serving tendencies fostered by contemporary society.

On April 12, 1984, 80,000 young athletes gathered from all over the world at the Olympic Stadium in Rome for the International Jubilee for Athletes. Their "sport's manifesto" declared:

> Sport is at the service of people and not people at the service of sport, and therefore the dignity of the human person is the goal and criterion of all sporting activity. . . . Sport is sincere and generous confrontation, a meeting place, a bond of solidarity and friendship . . . Sport can be genuine culture when the setting in which it is practiced and the experience that it brings are open and sensitive to human and universal values for the balanced development of the human person in all his or her dimensions.

What further encouragement do we need to enter into the fun of competing, of playing, of enjoying ourselves and of overcoming obstacles, of letting the pleasure of our acts be an antidote to the poison of disappointment and on-the-job tensions, softening the harsh blows of everyday life?

There is a determined thrust toward reform at the very heart of the physical-education establishment. The ranks of joggers, hikers, swimmers, and cyclists of all ages have mushroomed, and there are signs that increasing numbers of people are beginning to find words to express those magical values in sports that make mere winning seem empty indeed. We stand on the edge of the most exciting period in the history of athletics, a period of newly-awakened physical awareness, a period that better understands the meaning of wellness and genuine leisure. Something at the very heart of the athletic experience which has been sadly neglected in this culture is in the process of being uncovered and reclaimed. It requires only the eyes to see and the spirituality to appreciate the gift. We will need a finely tuned sense of harmony, for the art of reconciling and integrating these hitherto disparate elements within our lives starts, not in some distant place, but here, in my body and being and in yours.

Sports as a Doorway to the Transcendent

Athletics, in addition to flattening one's stomach and slimming one's hips, can change the way one lives and provide basic guidelines for lasting transformation of consciousness. The intensity of the experience, the intricacy of the relationships, the total involvement of body and senses, all come together in sports to create the precondition for those extraordinary events that culture calls "paranormal" or "mystical."

Such breakthrough experiences will only surprise those who see the world without benefit of an incarnational spirituality. The constant points of reference must be that we are created in God's own image, and that God has become flesh that we might become like God. No matter how fallen we are, redemption and transformation are readily and presently available. Everything in creation carries the message, most of all this flesh which harbored the Word itself.

In the face of this, it is not just war and disease and famine and obvious social injustices that appall us; it is also the pervasive waste of human potential. How is it that so many individual lives, bearing Godlike capacities themselves, are dedicated to deadening and demeaning pursuits? How is it, George Leonard asks in *The Ultimate Athlete* (Avon, 1974), that aware of transcendent possibilities in everyday activities, "we see God's image grub-bing and grabbing for meaningless consumer products" and "trivial quasi-artistic fads"?

Leonard's book, which is subtitled "Revisioning Sports, Physical Education, and the Body," puts forward the thesis that it is not as difficult as we think to alter our states of being. To do this is a natural human capacity. He uses sports as a framework for his reflections, referring to their "transformational aspects," that is, boundaries crossed, limitations transcended, and percep-tions gained. In citing the words of Shivas Irons, "You are a lucky man if you can find a strong, beautiful discipline, one that takes you beyond yourself," Leonard reflects that discipline, freely chosen, fully experienced, is one of those transformational ele-ments that has been neglected and even denigrated by our present culture. When the "mental" aspects of sports are given more at-tention and when the "mystical" aspects are allowed to rise from the underground to full awareness, then it is possible that new sports breakthroughs will become commonplace. It is on these as-pects of sports that our attention will be particularly focused in the remaining chapters.

The Ultimate Athlete in Leonard's definition is:

- one who joins body, mind, and spirit in the dance of exis-tence;
- one who explores both inner and outer being;
- one who surpasses limitations and crosses boundaries in the process of personal and social transformation;
- one who plays the larger game, the Game of Games, with full awareness, aware of life and death and willing to accept the pain and joy that awareness brings;
- one who, finally, best serves as model and guide on our evolutionary journey.

This ideal, which must remain tentative and open-ended, does not exclude anyone because of physical disabilities. In fact, the overweight, sedentary, middle-aged man or woman becomes a hero just by making a first laborious, agonizing circuit of the track. Six months or a year later, many pounds lighter, eyes glowing, that person may provide a model of the potential that exists in every one of us. To go a step further: if that same person, recognizably transformed in body, mind, and spirit, takes this experience as the impetus for further explorations and boundary crossings and the heightening of awareness, then he or she must be said to have embodied the ultimate athletic ideal. (pp. 287–288)

If Leonard's enthusiastic, futuristic outlook strikes us as idealistic evolutionary romanticism, the Zen philosophies being imported from the East and applied to various sporting activities promise to neutralize our skepticism and make believers of us all. The German philosopher Eugen Herrigel spent several years in Japan learning the art of archery and writes about it in *Zen in the Art of Archery* (Pantheon Books, 1953). By the "art" of archery he does not refer to the ability of the sportsperson, which can be more or less controlled by bodily exercises, but an ability whose origin is to be sought in spiritual exercises and whose aim consists in hitting a spiritual goal. Access to the art is only granted to those who are "pure" in heart, untroubled by subsidiary aims. It is worth noting the strong resonance between this and what we have said earlier about the true spirit of leisure and the value play has for its own sake.

All of the Japanese arts—ink painting, the tea ceremony, flower arrangement, swordsmanship, and archery—presuppose a spiritual attitude, an attitude which, in its most exalted form, is characteristic of Dhyana Buddhism known in Japan as "Zen."

Dhyana Buddhism was born in India and, after undergoing profound changes, reached full development in China, to be finally adopted by Japan where it is cultivated as a living tradition to this day. It has been credited with disclosing unsuspected ways of existence. At the heart of the Zen approach is an "immediate experience of what, as the bottomless ground of Being, cannot be apprehended by intellectual means, and cannot be conceived or interpreted by even the most unequivocable and incontestable experiences: one knows it by not knowing it'' (Herrigel, p. 21). With regard to the art of archery, the bow and arrow are only the instruments of essentially spiritual exercises which enable one to make a decisive leap toward a heightened and more lucid quality of experiencing life. The point is not to accomplish anything outwardly with bow and arrow, but only inwardly, with one's self.

The state described as ''spiritual'' by the Zen master is a state in which nothing definite is thought, planned, striven for, desired or expected; a state of mind which aims in no particular direction and yet knows itself capable alike of the possible and the impossible; a state which is at bottom purposeless and egoless. But because it is charged with spiritual awareness, it is called ''right presence of mind,'' which means that the mind or spirit is present everywhere, because it is nowhere attached to any particular place. And it can remain present because, even when related to this or that object, it does not cling to it by reflection and thus lose its original mobility. It has a seemingly mystical power because it is free, and it is open to everything because it is empty.

When the pupil risks getting stuck in the mire of his achievement, the master reminds him that all right doing is accomplished only in a state of true selflessness, and that more important than all outward works, however attractive, is the inward work which he has to accomplish if he is to fulfill his vocation as an artist.

The importance of the ''inner game'' is exemplified in one of the master's instructions to his pupils when their arrows flew off in the right direction but failed to hit even the sandbank, much less the target, and buried themselves in the ground just in front of it:

> Your arrows do not carry because they do not reach far enough spiritually. You must act as if the goal were infinitely

far off. For master archers it is a fact of common experience that a good archer can shoot further with a medium-strong bow than an unspiritual archer can with the strongest. It does not depend on the bow, but on the presence of mind, on the vitality and awareness with which you shoot. In order to unleash the full force of this spiritual awareness, you must perform the ceremony differently: rather as a good dancer dances. If you do this, your movements will spring from the center, from the seat of right breathing. Instead of reeling off the ceremony like something learned by heart, it will then be as if you were creating it under the inspiration of the moment, so that dance and dancer are one and the same. By performing the ceremony like a religious dance, your spiritual awareness will develop its full force. (p. 80)

The Zen language risks sounding esoteric to the Western ear to the point where it may seem to be talking about a realm of experience other than our own. I am convinced, however, that experiences described by the Zen master as ''spiritual'' are not foreign to us. We have had experiences of a state ''in which nothing definite is thought, planned, striven for, desired, or expected; a state of mind which aims in no particular direction and yet knows itself capable alike of the possible and the impossible.''

An example from my own experience is illustrative. The setting was the Minnesota State Track and Field Championship held at St. Thomas College in St. Paul. The preliminaries in one of my events, the hurdles, had been held in the morning and I had placed second in my heat, thereby qualifying for the finals in the early afternoon. During the noon hour I went to the dormitory room of a friend on campus, let myself in with a key he'd given me for that purpose, put a long-playing album of my favorite music on his stereo, and lay down on his bed. I spent the next hour in a state of deep relaxation.

When the time came for me to go back to the stadium, I felt reposed and peaceful. I was just looking forward to running.

There were three hurdlers in the finals whom I'd never beaten and whose times were consistently better than mine. I had no expectation of winning and was just happy to be there. It didn't even faze me when I drew the outside lane assignment, always a disadvantage because you can't tell where anyone else is until late in the race due to the staggered start. If you *can* tell, it means you're already far behind!

The official called us to our starting blocks. I remember feeling wonderfully loose and alert. The gun went off, and I never saw anyone until coming off the last hurdle. The fellow who appeared in the corner of my eye four lanes over was the one favored to win and there wasn't enough ground left for him to overtake me.

The memory I retain of that experience is of a compressed moment of fluidity. What was the key to it? In Zen language, I would say "right presence of mind." "A good archer can shoot further with a medium-strong bow than an unspiritual archer can with the strongest. It does not depend on the bow, but on the presence of mind, on the vitality and awareness with which you shoot."

In order to experience the full force of abundant life which is available to us, we must approach the ceremony of living as a good dancer dances, allowing it to spring from our center.

An Important Footnote to All of the Above

If one were drawing up a contract based on the above postulates toward the procuring of more and fuller life, there would undoubtedly be some fine print on the bottom of the page which would probably read something like this:

> Sports do not automatically and infallibly produce the benefits attributed to them in the field of human growth and development. They possess no magical powers. Neither do they

possess the pristine purity nor the recreative power nor the basic integrity which their ideologists all too easily attribute to them. Although they may afford those who so desire to engage in them with the favorable opportunity for acquiring certain personal qualities, they do not necessarily provide the internal and external conditions necessary for the promised success.

One finds that kind of disclaimer affixed to everything that promises anything. It has its place here, too: to remind those who read on that there is a wide spectrum of benefits available and that not everyone will have the same quality of experience.

At the very least, however, a regular, disciplined program of exercise promises a new perspective on life. That, in itself, is considerable. I do not consider the promise exaggerated for the following reason: regular exercise strengthens a person's physical, mental, and emotional stamina. When this happens, the quality of one's life is changed.

One could go further and cite less illness, longer life expectancy, reduced tension, better appearance, higher energy levels, increased imagination and creativity, more confidence and self-assurance. All are benefits regularly attested to. Can you think of anything else that could produce a more impressive short-list of qualities conducive to holistic health and wellness?

As John Carmody says in *Holistic Spirituality:*

Unless we use our bodies well, we ignore a major part of our identity. Unless we get ourselves into good shape, we never know how the world might look, sound, smell, taste, and feel. . . .

The dancer or well-trained actress knows things through, with, and in her body that pass the rest of us by. What for us is murky in perception or expression is for her clear and self-possessed. So she is the more lucid and enriched, we the muddier and poorer. For she has exercised her embodied self, while we have lounged and loafed. Our range of humanity is constricted. The potential God gave us is unplumbed. Once again those biblical talents become our accusers. How could we not know we were supposed to become lithe and well-conditioned? What master craftsman could make such a marvel as the human body and not be disappointed when we allow it to rust? Still, I would have the tone of these questions be more sorrow than outrage. These days outrage is too much with us, and too little profitable. Those ever earnest soon are ever tiresome, like rain falling on a tin roof. It is the edge of sadness that I would pry, the regret at another praise and joy being lost. (pp. 77–78)

Keeping Our Focus

The second half of this book takes up sporting activity in four of its expressions. I began to think concertedly about sporting activity as a place of encounter with God while participating in a month-long Outward Bound wilderness program in 1972. In paging through the journal I kept during that experience in which whitewater canoeing, rock climbing and cliff rappelling provided the context for an encounter with ourselves, our limits and our capacities, I find passages like the following:

> If the emphasis in theology today is validly placed on the vertical moving downward to the depths of the human; if we really believe that in depthing the feelings of normal everyday human existence—feelings of hurt, of joy, of confusion, of peace, of insecurity, of empathy and so on—there is a spiritual experience, then certainly forms of activity in which we have powerful and enthralling experiences have value and relevancy for our spiritual life and growth.

Elsewhere in my journal the following passage appears. It came as a reflection on some particularly taxing wilderness experiences which had caused me to redefine my physical and mental limits:

> I think I can honestly speak of a breakthrough and movement to dimensions of my own depths which I had not previously known. There has been something like a new birthing in me, and it has subtly nudged me into knowing a little more closely who I am constantly called to become. My human experience brought me to an experience of faith time and again, and I have found it most meaningful to relate Christ to that experience. If, as much of Christian anthropology is saying today, Christ is the apex of humanity; if in him we see the highest possibilities of what it means to be human; if full humanness is Christhood—then when I experience the potential in myself for fuller humanness and say "yes" to it, I am saying "yes" to Christ and his growth in me. It occurs to me that my wilderness sojourn (Outward Bound) has been in the mainstream of the direction theology is taking today as it ponders our human experience in an attempt to discover Christ.

The chapters to follow represent the evolution of this exploration, begun in that Outward Bound experience, to identify and set forth more clearly the points of connectedness between spirituality and sports. In an effort to make my thought as applied as possible, in chapters 5–8 I will take four of the most popular forms of sporting activity today and try to demonstrate how each enhances wellness, contributes to genuine leisure, and relates to one's spirituality.

The four activities chosen are all aerobic (literal translation: with air). Aerobic exercises are those which are the most efficient per time spent to improve physical fitness. An aerobic exercise is one which is steady and non-stop, is sustained for about fifteen minutes, maintains one's heart at 70–80 percent of its maximum for the entire time one is exercising, and is done at least three or four days a week.

I will not get into "how-to" concerns—there are scores of books available written by experts that will better serve those who are interested in knowing more about the basic skills involved in these sports. I will limit myself to the kind of reflection on those activities which is generally not found in the "how-to" books.

Athletic activities, because of their very physicalness, represent the ideal material for a sample application of an incarnationalist, creation-centered spirituality. In my approach to these activities I will try to do the following:

A: To approach athletic activities as contributing to an everexpanding experience of pleasurable and purposeful living especially as motivated by (and here I would add *contributing to*) spiritual values and religious beliefs;

B: To be especially attentive in these activities to the ways in which they embody characteristics of true leisure:
- does it nurture freedom of spirit?
- does it enable one to transcend the dimensions of economic and social necessity and to participate in experiences that are more qualitatively satisfying?
- does it heighten one's experience of the quality of life?
- does it yield sense and style to one's way of living?
- does it assist one in discovering the presence of grace and peace in one's daily walk?

As we have already seen in Chapter 3, the experience of inner-freedom or leisure is in direct relation to an incarnationalist spirituality which identifies more and fuller life as both our human and spiritual aim. Benefits of seeing a clearer line between one's bodily activities and one's spirituality can run in two directions:

1) For those who are very interested in their spiritual growth and development, such a clearer vision can
   a. help them look upon athletic leisure activities with new eyes and a new appreciation of the contribution these activ-

ities can make toward a holistic-incarnational spirituality—
one that not only accepts but positively celebrates bodiliness. As we noted in Chapter 2, our thanks are genuine only
when we use the gifts we have been given in the way they
were intended to be received: as life enhancing. Thus:

b. encourage their rightful use of the gift (bodiliness) which
    enables them to enjoy life to the full and
c. help them further their spiritual growth and development by
    expanding the sphere of where and how they pursue that
    goal.

2) For those who are already engaged in one or more forms of
    sports but who do not consider themselves "religious," seeing
    the benefits that flow from their involvement not only in the
    normally stated terms of "weight and stress control, etc." but
    also in terms of their spiritual life may help them
    a. to accept and feel more comfortable with the vital dimen-
        sions of their lives which to this point they have been hard
        put to see in any meaningful terms;
    b. to see their sports activities as a gateway through which
        they might embark on a conscious and positive develop-
        ment of the life-enhancing potential available to them
        through a spirituality that prizes their bodily experiences;
    c. to appreciate their "breakthrough" experiences as a taste
        of the kind of harmonious, satisfying, fulfilling living
        which is our Creator's offer to and wish for us.

In whichever direction the enrichment flows, the overall results will be the same: an enhanced quality of living by means of
a deeper integration of *all* the dimensions of one's life. In one
word: wellness. In two words: abundant life.

In short, what follows is an effort to do "applied theology."
Theological reflection, unless it touches down in people's lives,
unless it comes at them in terms understandable and meaningful

to them by virtue of what engages them, will never heighten the quality of their lives or result in more and fuller life. You may be surprised to find in what I say that it is not all God-talk. That is because the point from which I begin is not that we must ''make people religious,'' but that we already are religious in the very depths of our being and only need to uncover it and value it. The result can only bring one closer to the goal of our human existence: more and fuller life. If one foot is nature, the other is grace, and the only way to live is to walk!

Chapter 5

Running

"I believe that God made me for a purpose. . . . But he also made me *fast*. And when I run, I feel his pleasure. You were right; it is fun. But that isn't all. . . . "

Eric Little
in *Chariots of Fire*

A recent highlight was one of the most fun runs I have ever enjoyed. It started off on a course that took me through a woodland park, then down a long hill to another park where there is a small lake and a waterfowl preserve. At one point, I stopped along the lake just to enjoy the antics of the ducks and the geese. Then I continued to a spring-fed pond about a mile away, and took off my shoes and shirt and jumped in for a swim. I let the sun and the breeze dry me off while meditating on the beach for about a half an hour. Then I pulled my shoes and shirt back on and turned my steps toward home, stopping for a few minutes along the way to watch an inning of a Little League baseball game. After deciding that not much besides the uniforms and the equipment had improved in the twenty-five years since my Little League days, I took off across a long grassy field, still wet and soggy from the rain the evening before. Once on the road again, my own favorite mind-fantasy was working well—picking out a telephone pole about a quarter of a mile down the road, and imagining one end of a rope tied around my waist and the other around the telephone pole, I let it reel me in. In the last three-quarters of a mile, the effects of the swim, the warm sun, and the long, leisurely run all came together into a marvelous sense of harmony, flow, and glide. Lying on the grass under a couple of big maple trees, I simply enjoyed the sense of well-being, watching the sunlight filtering through and playing upon the leaves above.

We are happy when, however briefly, we become one with ourselves, others and the world of nature. And sport, as Dr. George Sheehan attests, provides such moments:

> Some of the good things in play are physical grace, psychological ease and personal integrity. The best are the peak experiences, when you have a sense of oneness with yourself and nature. . . . It may be that the hereafter will have them in constant supply. I hope so. But while we are in the here and now, play is the place to find them—the place where we are constantly being and becoming ourselves (*On Running*, Bantam Books, 1978, p. 189).

Our series of applied reflections begins with running because running, as George Leonard has noted in *The Ultimate Athlete*, is the essence of most sports played on dry land. Soccer, baseball, basketball, football, rugby, cricket, field-hockey, frisbee, various forms of tag—all of these might be viewed as just so many complicated excuses for running. Further, javelin throwing, pole vaulting, and long jumping begin with and depend on running. Squash, handball, and tennis involve a series of short sprints. Dance is built around the esthetic possibilities of the run and the leap. The land sports which include no running are few in number.

When one strips land sports of all the rules and complications that give them their separate characteristics, the essence remains, and the essence is running itself: pure, unadorned running. Perhaps the ultimate sport. Running may offer us agony, climax, and transcendence, but it also is a simple, healthy exercise—probably the cheapest and most readily-available way of improving circulation, breathing, and general muscle tone. While helping to connect us to other forms of existence, running is also a way of increasing our chances of survival in this one.

At a scientific conference a few years ago, a psychiatrist speculated upon the depth of running's imprint on our genetic consciousness. "If it is true," he said, "that the human being is the greatest long-distance land animal on our planet—that is, that a human can run down any other land animal—this indicates that there may be a biological or evolutionary pattern or archetype which resonates to very deep levels of our unconscious."

William Glasser, M.D., in building his theory of positive addiction in a book by the same name (Harper and Row, 1976), agrees. He believes that running creates the optimal condition for positive addiction (a notion which we shall further explore later on) because it is the most ancient and still most effective survival mechanism. We are descended from those who ran to stay alive and this need to run is programmed genetically into our brains. When we have gained the endurance to run long distances easily, then a good run reactivates the ancient neural program. As this occurs we reach a stage of mental preparedness that leads to a basic feeling of satisfaction.

The man credited with triggering philosophical reflection about running is Dr. George Sheehan. There is strong resonance between many of the themes he treats in his book *On Running* (Bantam Books, 1975) and those which have been set forth in these pages. Dr. Sheehan speaks of how the body mirrors the soul and the mind, and is much more accessible than either. Therefore, it makes good sense to become proficient at listening to one's body in order that one might eventually hear from one's totality— from the complex, unique person that one is.

"I discovered that my body was a marvelous thing, and learned that any ordinary human can move in ways that have excited painters and sculptors since time began," writes Dr. Sheehan. "In the creative action of running, I became convinced of my own importance, certain that my life had significance" (pp. 4–5). He testifies that with the increase of awareness and sensual connection that he has experienced with everything around him through the act of running, his existence has been enlarged, that because of running he is now living more abundantly. Running gave him the insight that he was only using a small part of his mental and physical resources. He does not, however, avoid the tension between what he recognizes he is and what he perceives he can be, but allows that tension to be a creative lever toward more and fuller life. Running has become important in his life because he has discovered that as one completes oneself physically, it benefits one *totally*. Since the energies exist to accomplish this, the real problem is to discover how these energy reserves can be tapped.

One of the people who bemoaned the gap between the absence of disease on the one hand, and true *joie de vivre* with all its energy, vitality and well-being on the other hand, was Lt. Gen. R. L. Bohannon, M.D., founder of the National Jogging Association in the late 1960's. His approach was straightforward and understandable to all: "Jogging is the simplest, cheapest, least encumbered, most available and most efficient way to build up the heart and lungs."

Some years later, Air Force doctor Kenneth Cooper set millions of people to jogging with his carefully researched book *Aerobics* (M. Evans & Co., 1968), claiming he was practicing "preventive medicine." Aerobic exercises are those which are the most efficient per time spent to improve physical fitness. An aerobic exercise is one which is steady and non-stop, is sustained for about 15 minutes, maintains one's heart at 70–80 percent of its maximum for the entire time one is exercising, and is done at least three or four days a week. Frequency, Intensity, Time (FIT) became key aerobic principles.

And so the fitness movement grew, with running as its centerpiece. The message to an increasingly body-conscious North American public was blunt: use it or lose it. Running gained advocates by the millions because it pays off, and it pays off in a very short time. The exhilarating effects are only weeks away, and as Dr. Sheehan says, "There is a natural high to be obtained legally." The Olympic ideal of *citius, altius, fortius* (swifter, higher, stronger) is addressed to everyone. It is, ultimately, a question of growth, of *being* more. The growing strength that one feels within a month of jogging three times weekly for twenty minutes each time is as spiritual and intellectual as it is physical.

Let's Be Realistic

I agree with Joan Ullyot, M.D., when she states in *Running Free* (G. P. Putnam's Sons, 1980) that too much publicity about various mystical states or "runner's high" can be misleading. The average beginning runner is more worried about getting around the block on a daily basis than about enlightenment. Search for meaning "beyond running" may be fine, but not before one can handle the jogging alone without undue strain. The beginner will go through profound physiological and anatomical changes. Muscles unused for years will protest. The would-be runner will wonder if this pain is normal and if it will ever pass. He will not be in a religious mood. And the beginner may only be discouraged to read ecstatic accounts of transcendental experiences on the run. She may even quit, convinced that running can't be for her, because of the pain and effort she feels.

Thus it is perhaps best to say unequivocally at the outset that simply getting caught up in the pure and simple act of running is its own benefit. There are safer ways to exercise than this, better ways to meditate, quicker ways to get high, truer ways to find religion, easier ways to have fun. While I believe that running does give some of these things, I do not want to so focus on the potential positive aspects as to deny that it is a sport like all sports and thus has both pain and joy, risk and reward.

If any further disclaimer is needed, perhaps it suffices to say that we all know people who are runners and who are not saints! We may have even witnessed moments when they became just a little too aggressive in their criticism of people who smoke, eat junk food and get fat. We may have witnessed them flaunt their fitness to the point of making other people uncomfortable. It is not without a certain foundation in personal experience that many North Americans have concluded that running is a monumental nuisance and runners themselves relentless bores. Arnold Bennett enumerates some of the dangers of life in his book *How To Live on 24 Hours a Day* and one of them is becoming a prig: "A prig is a tedious individual who, having made a discovery, is so impressed by it that he is capable of being gravely displeased because the entire world is not also impressed with it." You may know some jogger who has fallen prey to this "danger of life."

What needs to be recognized is that running, like feelings, is morally neutral, is not good or bad. What makes it either of positive or of negative value is the place it has in one's life. Jumping from one foot to the other is only as good or as bad as the meaning one gives to it and the ends to which one puts it. What can be said with certainty is this: the more one understands and directs the reasons for running, the more one will benefit from it.

Finally, it is not everyone's sport, and one must take one's body-build and psychological needs into consideration when choosing the proper kind of sporting activity. Some people need contests in which self-quest figures highly, and others need games which are a classroom in interpersonal relationships. Depending on the individual, those games may have to be games of chance or skill or strategy. Each one must find the art forms which fit best. Running, swimming, skiing, and dancing are just a few of the possibilities. Although there are special reasons why I chose to treat of these, it would also have been possible to focus on cycling, canoeing, or the martial arts.

Getting Started

When you first start to run, be very gentle and kind to yourself. Be sensitive to your feelings. Ideally, run in a beautiful place—through the woods, around a lake or along a river. Before starting your run, spend at least ten minutes doing gentle stretching exercises. Treat your body with the care that an artist does in working with his or her material. Jog at a pace where you're breathing hard but are not out of breath, not straining anything in your body. Dr. Kenneth Cooper's advice to beginning joggers is to go immediately to three miles or thirty minutes, whichever comes first. And stay there. Repeat the session at least every other day. Walk some, most, or all at first, if that's the only way to finish comfortably. There's no need to constantly push yourself past your limits; just go out and start moving. If a slow jog is still too fast for conversation, you have to start with a walk instead. As time goes on, your exercise will become much easier. The decreasing scale of time it takes you to cover the same distance is much less important than your overall mental, spiritual, and physical health. Cooper's typical run lasts considerably less than thirty minutes, and he has mountains of data to prove that this is enough to maintain physical fitness.

He writes in his latest book, *The Aerobics Program for Total Well-Being:* "Recent research has shown that unless a person is training for marathons or other competitive events, it's best to limit running to around twelve to fifteen miles per week. More than that will greatly increase the incidence of joint and bone injuries, and other ailments. On the other hand, less mileage (than 12–15 per week) will fail to achieve the desired improvement in the body" (quoted in *Runners' World,* June 1984, p. 55). For non-racers, Cooper sets minimums and maximums: no less than two miles, four times a week; and no more than three miles five days a week. He and his staff at the Aerobic Center in Dallas have been overwhelmed by the injury rates in people running more than twenty-five miles a week. While a competitor may willingly take the risks associated with higher mileage, Cooper says it first yields diminishing returns and eventually negative ones.

Herbert A. deVries, former director of the physiology of exercise laboratory at the Andrus Gerontology Center at the University of Southern California and the author of *Fitness After 50,* says: "There are many middle-age and older people who can get by putting in a lot of miles. But there are also many who cannot. It's a very individual thing, but we have to be careful recommending anything for a mass of people in which even a few could get hurt. For the average person in his 50's, 60's or 70's—and I'm talking about people who are running to improve their health, not to compete in marathons—we ought not to be recommending any more than three miles every other day."

Cooper is convinced that a person who is exercising regularly is psychologically healthier than the person who is not involved in a regular physical activity program. "Control is expensive," says the psychiatrist in the film *Ordinary People,* yet self-mastery, autonomy, and control—all the things a psychiatrist prescribes yet finds so difficult to dispense—are reported by a great deal of runners. To come by those qualities, along with identity and self-esteem, the cost is just an hour four times a week. Can you find a better bargain than that?

A report from psychiatrists at the University of Arizona describes runners as generally "self-effacing, hard-working, high achievers." There is hardly a teacher or an employer who would not prefer this kind of person. "Assuming an identity as a runner," the report continues, "serves an adaptive function, providing a sense of self, a feeling of control over internal and external circumstances and a difficult but attainable goal." Testimonies like these are what cause Dr. George Sheehan to claim, "Running *is* therapy."

Dr. Richard Steiner, a pathologist-marathoner, says, "Long distance running can give you a teenage cholesterol, remodel your lungs, lower your blood pressure, and slow your pulse." In addition to cleaning his arteries, he also believes it cleans his mind and soul. The basis for such a claim is that the brain cannot function at anything close to maximum power unless the body is in excellent condition. Intellectual health depends on the proper circulation of blood to the brain where are located both our mental activities and the seat of our personalities. Thus, the importance of keeping it healthy and free from the disadvantages of poor physiological and psychological functions, and from defects of blood supply due to obstruction of the arteries. Scores of scientists have verified the truth that mental ability almost invariably increases as physical fitness improves. Moreover, running and other high-intensity activities bring a number of other far-reaching psychological changes. Someday, scientists may be able to explain why these changes occur. When they do, they will only be telling our minds what our bodies in their intuitive wisdom have already known.

With all the positive aspects of running, there is still room for concern, even on the level of fitness. Most people who are running today think running and physical fitness are synonymous. We have not been talking here about marathon runners, but let's take them as an example. Most of the spectators who stand in the streets and cheer or who sit at home and drink beer while watching the New York City or Boston Marathon on television are envious of the apparent physical fitness demonstrated by the thousands of runners. Most of the runners will be thinking that they are in the best physical condition of their lives. But the fitness that most of them have is limited. They are fit to run the marathon, which is admirable, but that is not total physical fitness.

A good number of those marathon finishers, if they were to play three games of raquetball, would be so stiff in the arms, shoulders, upper back and legs that they would want to stay in bed the next morning after they had played. While their cardiovascular or aerobic fitness is excellent, they have given little attention to upper-body fitness, the muscles in the arms and shoulders and upper-back.

Total physical fitness includes muscular strength, endurance and flexibility. Many people are concentrating so much on running to develop their aerobic fitness that they are neglecting muscular fitness and flexibility in their quest to develop a strong heart and healthy lungs. However, they fail to understand that muscular strength, endurance and flexibility are important for maintaining a healthy, upright posture and to avoid musculo-skeletal problems such as low-back pain. The concept of total physical fitness is especially important in the growth and development of young people. We should not encourage them to specialize in activities that will favor either aerobic fitness or muscular fitness to the exclusion of the other.

It is for this reason that I favor running programs which are divided into three parts, such as suggested by Mike Spino in *Beyond Jogging* (Celestial Arts, 1976): 65% for improving endurance, 25% for developing tempo or speed, and 10% resistance training to build body strength. Aerobic endurance (or stamina) training builds muscle tone and strengthens the cardiovascular system, just as jogging does. Speed training increases the body's ability to use oxygen. The final 10% of the fitness program is for developing muscle and skeletal power. Consequently, running alone can never be the answer. Resistance, i.e. putting the muscles through a series of efforts against resistance, is often overlooked in conditioning programs. Thus, push-ups or weights or isometric exercises using anything immovable (door lintel, side of the house, dresser) has a place. This total approach to fitness was impressed upon me when I was coaching high school track in California by the distance-coach who never failed to have his runners get down on the grass and do push-ups at the end of their distance workout.

Women Hit the Road

"Changing Times: Women and Physical Activity" is the name of a survey conducted in Canada and made public in October, 1984. The Canadian Fitness Survey, based on twenty-two thousand questionnaires and sixteen thousand fitness tests conducted in 1981, revealed that although most Canadian women of all ages are active, they do not exercise hard enough to get fit. It warned that women's stamina, muscular endurance, flexibility and body composition are not adequate.

"It is important," the survey said, "to encourage females to expand their choices to include activities in each season and to help girls and women design a year-round exercise program." While the results were generally encouraging in that they showed that more women were active in 1981 than they were in 1976, the survey nonetheless concluded that only a minority of women over forty have the recommended fitness level. "Fitness leaders and programmers," the survey directed, "must therefore devise programs that will help females increase their participation *and* improve each component of fitness."

One of the areas of fitness activity that has seen a tremendous influx in the number of women participants is running. In Jim Fixx's *Second Book of Running* (Random House, 1978), he notes that an investment company that was thinking of financing a running magazine calculated that women were taking up running at a rate as much as 30% greater than the rate for men.

Joan Ullyot thinks that women have a much better chance psychologically of evolving into runners than men. The reason she gives is that women run realistically whereas men run romantically. That is to say, women grasp the concept of pacing, whereas most men can't seem to restrain themselves.

> The ability of most women to run at an enjoyable pace, without guilt, is probably responsible for the number of women flocking to running in recent years. The sport is unregulated and need not be competitive. It can be anything you choose to make of it. Each run can be fast or slow, relaxation or challenge, depending on your own wishes. A woman can grasp this concept in the first jog, when her own breathing tells her whether to run faster or to walk. The older male runner, taught to run hard and fast without regard to the feelings of his own body, may take months to overcome this early brainwashing. Some never learn how. Some continue to feel that enjoyment is somehow, well . . . *unmanly*. (*Running Free,* p. 45)

So, whereas men think of themselves as the realists (strong, silent, level-headed), it is women who use their heads much better to compensate for raw power. Ullyot, a pioneer of the running movement and one of its most significant writers, believes that running fosters the same traits in women that enabled their pioneer foremothers to hold the frontier together: calm, dependability, self-reliance, toughness and resilience. The longer, harder, and more challenging the distance or race, she claims, the more obvious becomes the female doggedness and imperturbability. In the non-runner, such qualities have been buried, hidden under the fluttery emotional facade—for women still try to *appear* romantic and to live up to their accepted stereotype.

Ernst Van Aaken, the great German doctor/coach, concurs. He considered women the true endurance athletes. He once wrote:

> Psychologically, men are more explosive, inconstant, not enduring, and in pain and exertion—especially among high-performance athletes—somewhat snivelling. Women are the opposite: tough, constant, enduring, level and calm under the pain to which their biology exposes them (during childbirth). On the average, women are more patient than men. Armed with these advantages, women are in a position to do endurance feats previously considered impossible.

Once past a trial-and-error period in training, women generally exhibit incredible tenacity. They are less eager to put undue stress on their bodies, and are content to enjoy the running for its own sake, rather than for improving distance or time.

Moreover, the psychological changes that Dr. Ullyot describes from those who take up running are much more pronounced in women than in men. The men in her groups tended to lose weight, gain endurance and change their wardrobe, but apart from that, they seemed to be the same after conditioning as before.

The changes in women, however, went beyond the physical realm. Besides slimming down and becoming fit, besides replacing pale skin with a natural health-glow and a sparkle in the eyes, there were important personality changes. Those who started out somewhat insecure, and self-deprecating acquired a new confidence. First they could run one mile, then three! The former impossibility had become a reality. They began to wonder what else they could do that they had always considered impossible.

> If a mile is possible, anything may be possible. She feels herself a physical creature perhaps for the first time since early childhood. She feels competent, in control of her life. If she becomes a marathoner, she no longer worries about being stranded twenty miles from her home with a flat tire—if worst comes to worst, she can always run home. If she is stranded in the mountains, she can hike out. She begins to suspect, *if there is anything* she is told she can't do because she's a woman, that she is being fed a line. (*Running Free*, p. 64)

Psychologically, the increasing sense of self-mastery helps toward overcoming possible patterns of self-denial, masochism, and weakness that so many of us unfortunately still find deeply embedded in our psyches. Giving up these negative patterns can have as great an impact on health and vitality as the physical effects of the training. Once women take charge of disciplining their bodies, they often take a quantum leap in their level of self-expression.

Since women today over twenty were generally raised on the dogma that they were not capable of most physical performances expected of men, such discoveries of their own potential can amount to a renaissance of the spirit. Since we men have not come out of that cultural matrix, it is difficult for us to comprehend the profound impact that physical accomplishment can have on the average woman over twenty. A husband may not recognize, understand or appreciate the new creature his wife is becoming. The simple fact that my sister-in-law is running a marathon this coming weekend reminds me that my self-esteem must locate itself elsewhere than in being able to run faster, throw farther or climb higher than a woman.

The shifts taking place in men's and women's relationships with each other ask deep questions about our spirituality or our view of the world and the place of *all* people in it. It also brings into sharp focus the root meaning of leisure as freedom: leisure-as-freedom is realized when a person experiences more fully his or her own uniqueness and worth. A person finds leisure, for example, when she discovers who she is, what she can do with her life, and the abundance of happy circumstances, possibilities and relationships in which her life is cast. This experience of freedom is a quality of life that can be experienced during times of work as well as times of play and provides one's life with growing sense and new style.

Creative Approaches to Running

The New Age approach to sports deemphasizes competitive tendencies and invites the participant to enjoy the experience itself rather than just focusing on "getting there." Dyveke Spino and Ann Spence, in an article entitled "Creative Running: Tips from a New Age Coach" (*Holistic Health Lifebook,* And/Or Press, 1978, pp. 111–115), approached running as an activity filled with fun and imagination-play. Since psychological research indicates that images in the mind are relayed to the body, influencing mood, energy, feelings and actions, they suggest the use of positive images and fantasies which will put one in a good mood and generate extra energy. What follows gives a small taste:

- Imagine your feet are coming down on air puffs
- When running up a hill, imagine there is a giant hand pushing you from behind
- Connect an imaginary stream of light to a tree and let it pull you up the hill

- If running with a partner, imagine a stream of energy connecting your shoulders to each other, and take turns being in the lead and being equal; the dance of energy exchange breaks down patterns of power
- When running with a group, visualize a sun star over your heads, and then send out a network of light-streamers to hook up to this imaginary sun star. This sets up an energy field which pulls along the weakest members of the group without strain or injury, all the while giving a sense of interconnectedness among the members of the group
- Let your eyes become soft and slightly out of focus while running; this opens up the sensitivity of your other means of perception and intuitive senses. Look about 30 feet ahead of you, and let your feet begin to find their own way
- Let the wind gently push you along, and the sun fill your body with soft, golden energy
- Look at a tree in the distance and feel its energy, letting that energy pull you toward it
- Treat certain rocks or shrubs as friends which welcome you on your way
- For that 25% of your program that involves tempo and speed variation, run backward, sideways, jump and twirl
- Treat yourself occasionally to a steam bath and a massage
- Keep a journal of the different things you experience while running

New Age running will place increasingly greater emphasis on the receptive and intuitive aspects of our personalities. The so-called "feminine" or affective dimension will be increasingly valued. Competition, say Spino and Spence, will be viewed more and more as an out-moded value of an industrial age. In the future, the goal will be to awaken the spirit to higher and higher levels of personal transformation. Coaches, take notice: the developing job description is to be an inspirer of the soul, awakening the dreamer, the poetic, the heroic.

Television spectators of the 1984 Winter Olympics in Sarajevo, Yugoslavia, were given repeated examples of this new emphasis, even at the level of Olympic-class athletes, when various American and Canadian athletes were interviewed. Cross-country skier Bill Koch said: "The more I win, the more I believe that what's important isn't the winning but trying to do your best." Phil Mahre shrugged off a non-medal finish in his first slalom race by saying this wasn't the most important event of his life. He was winning the last race of the Olympics while his wife was delivering their first child at home. At a press conference, Mahre was asked which meant more to him—the gold medal or the birth of his son. He glared at the reporter and replied, "That's the dumbest question I've ever heard." Later in the interview session, Mahre got the chance to speak for all athletes who think that simply taking part still means something. "I came here with thoughts of skiing up to my potential," he said. "The unfortunate thing about the Olympics is that everyone rates them by the medals."

Running and Transformation of Consciousness

The creative approaches to running described above, with their pronounced use of mental imagery, indicate how within the past few years the mental aspects of running are one of psychology's most promising frontiers, one beyond which lie not only uncharted physiological and psychological territories but fundamental philosophical issues as well. If, for example, we ultimately confirm that human beings experience maximum psychological integrity when they exercise strenuously rather than when they are largely inactive, this finding would clearly suggest the sort of life humankind was in effect designed for. It would also suggest how far most of us have allowed ourselves to drift from our intended path.

James Fixx notes how we now live in the twilight of the Industrial Revolution's long first phase, the period in which our machines have been unable to function without physical effort on our part. Now, in the second phase, when computers and robots are beginning to perform all these functions, we are left with only one role at which we continue to excel: thought. If the evidence builds that humankind requires, in its fundamental nature, strenuous movement in order to have the greatest clarity of thought, it may be that only our play—running or some physically demanding substitute—will enable us to constructively guide the evolutionary life of this planet.

It has now been abundantly verified by numerous studies that runners are more likely than other athletes to experience striking psychological alterations. We simply do not yet know much about why running has such a profound effect on the human mind. For the moment all we know is that the experiences are real and considerably broader than even the most daring researchers suspected in the early days of the current running movement.

Fixx refers to 40 or more full-scale studies of exercise and personality alone, indicating that the literature is filled with hundreds of reports on exercise and mental health, exercise and intelligence, and exercise and other aspects of human psychology. From these studies, excellent new evidence exists that running in itself contributes to mental health. Although no one understands exactly why, ''people who run seem to call into being an otherwise elusive internal direction finder that guides them away from psychological distress.''

The precise mechanisms by which running affects us so deeply are still being investigated and debated. There are several theories: a) the changes result from nothing more than an elevated body temperature or an increase in the brain's blood supply; b) the changes are brought on by running's hypnotically repetitive rhythms; c) the changes result from the release of morphine-like chemicals called endorphins or from a natural stimulant called norepinephrine.

All that being what it may, the bottom line is that running

makes for more happy, fulfilled people. For a great many people who are exploring their potential, trying to become more fully what they are, running is instrumental in bringing new and fuller life, a higher level of wellness. As such, it is assisting them in realizing their human and spiritual aim.

The only approach we need to take to sport is the approach William James took to religion. The real backbone of the religious life, said James, was *experience*. Not philosophy or science. No *philosophy* of religion, he contended, could begin an adequate translation of what goes on in the single private human being.

Setting the Mind Spinning Free

In Chapter 3, we noted how leisure should be seen in terms of free spirit rather than free time, how leisure is the freedom which enables us to transcend those aspects of our lives which tend to weigh us down, how it is a foretaste of eternity rather than a particle of time. Leisure, as we have defined it, is essentially a spiritual experience rooted in a world view that sees more and fuller life as both a human and a spiritual aim. To the extent that we can further this development of the inner experience of freedom by means of a positive appreciation of our condition in the world—as spirited flesh—we are on the way to holistic health or wellness.

One of the particular characteristics of leisure—the freedom which enables us to transcend the dimensions of economics and social necessity and participate in higher realities—has been the object of concerted study and reflection by Dr. William Glasser, M.D. The phrases he uses to describe what I am convinced is the same reality we have described above are "the mind spins free" or one "goes out of one's mind." Dr. Glasser was first interested in this phenomenon when a man in one of his seminars described his experience of running as a process of letting his mind go, of letting his mind spin free. "Your mind is there," he said, "but it is not there—it's in sort of a transcendental, trance-like state."

After that encounter, Glasser talked with many other people who run regularly, and found that almost all of them describe a similar state of mind: a trance-like, transcendental mental state that accompanies the exercise. Glasser termed this state of mind "Positive Addiction." His subsequent research led him to conclude that meditators (who reach this state directly) and runners (who reach it indirectly) are the two largest identifiable groups of "positive addicts." By no means, however, were running and meditation the only means by which one could arrive at this state of mind. A positive addiction in Glasser's terms can be anything at all that a person chooses to do as long as it fulfills the following six criteria:

(1) It is something non-competitive that you choose to do and you can devote approximately an hour a day to it.

(2) It is possible for you to do it easily and it does not take a great deal of mental effort to do it well.

(3) You can do it alone or rarely with others but it does not depend upon others to do it.

(4) You believe that it has some value (physical, mental, or spiritual) for you.

(5) You believe that if you persist at it you will improve, but this is completely subjective—you need to be the only one who measures that improvement.

(6) The activity *must* have the quality that you can do it *without criticizing yourself. If you can't accept yourself during this time, the activity will not be addicting.* This is

why it is so important that the activity can be done alone. Anytime you introduce other people you chance introducing competition or criticism, often both. (*Positive Addiction,* p. 93)

What it is important for our purposes to realize is that this mental state where the mind "spins free" is available to everyone. It is not limited to any age brackets or to any particular activities. Glasser's research leads him to say that the only condition is that you usually have to do it for several months, sometimes for years.

Glasser notes that the "addiction" to running does not come quickly. It rarely happens until the runner has built enough endurance so that "he can run effortlessly for an hour." From this derives his statement that for most this takes at least six months and for many longer.

While one can reach this mental state through other activities, Glasser is convinced that running has a certain edge. At the outset of this chapter, I cited Glasser's conviction that the need to run is programmed genetically into our brains as an ancient and still effective survival mechanism. Because this activity is so programmed in the ancient pathways of our brains, when we run without fatigue and without self-criticism we are able to free most of the brain for other activity. When this happens, it is easy to slip into the euphoric, "out-of-one's-mind" state. Further, Glasser is convinced that modern men and women, amidst the stresses of contemporary civilization, have greater need for periods in which our minds "spin free" than did our primitive forebears. He concludes that if we can get these moments through running, we would be foolish not to consider this possibility, especially if we are finding it difficult to cope with any aspect of our lives. In other words, we have a need to "get out of our heads" at regular intervals, to engage in activities in which our brains are almost superfluous to the activity.

With optimum fitness, altered states of consciousness are possible. As an individual becomes more fit, he or she spends less time concentrating on the physical activity and has the possibility of transcending this level of consciousness and entering into another. The new state the mind enters when one is in excellent condition and running freely is in some ways similar to the mental state that characterizes meditation.

What happens during meditation? A person allows his or her mind to experience a relaxed state in which the attention is drawn inward. Whereas our daily experience is made up of an unending cascade of thoughts, emotions, sensations and perceptions, meditation provides for two brief daily periods of effortless disengagement from these continuous impressions. As the attention shifts inward, one experiences a state in which the mind becomes very quiet, but extraordinarily alert. One ceases to be conscious of this or that object and becomes consciousness itself. This consciousness is the ground and essential condition for experiencing. The more one meditates, the more one increases in consciousness and therefore in the ability to experience. Meditation is simply the technique which turns the mind in the right direction—toward the center, or basis of experience that is within. Meditation creates a space in time where creation fulfills the law of its being: to awaken to its Source.

That space in time is our human consciousness, unimaginably privileged to share in the being of God. It is not enough to talk *about* the mystery of God when it is our privilege to talk from *within* the heart of that Mystery where we are led by the Spirit. The Eastern Fathers of the Church thought that the only knowledge we can have of God is by *participation* in God's own self-knowledge. The establishing of the reign of God by Jesus is not to be seen just in terms of the presence of God, for God has always been present. The kingdom is established when one experiences God, when one shares in the very being of God. It is not a contact we can have from the outside, touching God as an object, but only from within God. To be open to God is to enter into communion with God's consciousness, unlimited and fully human.

It is a kind of "being to being" conversation. No words are needed. Nothing in between. To know God at this level is to have a real grasp of reality. It will influence the rest of our lives and our conduct. The ripe fruit of this prayer is to bring back into the humdrum routine of our ordinary lives, not just the *thought* of God, but the *awareness* of God's presence. As this awareness takes over a larger and larger part of one's day, there is nothing to possess and everything to be. In the final analysis, one meditates because this is simply the way to be. One meditates because God is. And being in communion with God gives glory to God. The real work is the work of oneing, of realizing the latent state of communion that is everywhere offered.

There are, to be sure, a number of highly beneficial side-effects. Physiological research has demonstrated that the reduction of mental activity which takes place in meditation results in a simultaneous reduction of the metabolism of the nervous system. This in turn brings about a state of profound relaxation, in which deeply-rooted stresses are eliminated. The regenerative changes throughout the entire nervous system are strikingly similar in meditation and running. Though these changes result from stress release, they necessarily involve whatever physical activity (e.g. running) is required to accomplish the change. Furthermore, the notion of our minds "spinning free," or of "getting out of our heads" at regular intervals to enter into another level of consciousness strongly suggests that running, like meditation, can be a "trigger mechanism technique" which opens the door to the experience of communion. What one has in those moments of "spinning free" is an experience of *awareness*. What one experiences first of all is one's own consciousness, one's own being. From there it is only a step to realize the Infinite, Incomprehensible, Ineffable One, at the center of one's being.

Glasser's research is just one more confirmation that we do have within us potentials which, if tapped, open up new and profound experiences of more abundant living. We can only wonder why more people do not explore these potentials—gifts to which we all have access.

There are certainly different reasons why people do not avail themselves of the resources at hand. We have spoken of running as one way of tapping into latent potential; it is not difficult to understand why for many it holds little attraction. Some give it a try and then drop out because they have attempted too much at once. Or they run in awful places. Or there are too many barking dogs who chase in the neighborhood.

But more often than not it is simply a question of not being able to get up in the morning or to carry through on one's resolve at the end of a day's work. There is no question about it: it takes discipline, as any runner knows. It means carving out an hour in the day and protecting it. Life is a gift. But experiencing this gift in abundance will never come if one only waits passively for it. Jesus tells us to set our heart on the kingdom. Setting our hearts on something involves not only serious aspiration but also strong determination. The forces that keep pulling us back from an experience of life as freedom and promise into a worry-filled existence are not easy to overcome. "How hard it is," Jesus exclaims, ". . . to enter the kingdom of God!" (Mark 10:23).

We are face to face with the role of discipline in the spiritual life. Discipline is the other side of discipleship. The spiritual life, whether cultivated through Scripture reading, running, or meditation, is impossible without discipline. Dom John Main, a teacher of Christian meditation, repeatedly said to me, "The most important thing is to be faithful and persevere."

I'll never forget an experience while working one summer at the Paulist Center in Boston as a seminarian. Many of the staff members were gone on a particular weekend, and one of the priests presided and preached at all five of the liturgies. He appeared to have as much energy and enthusiasm at the last one as he did at the first, and I couldn't help wondering how he did it. When I expressed my amazement to him about it afterwards, he simply said: "That's one of the reasons why I run faithfully several times a week. It helps me develop the stamina the ministry demands." I've never forgotten that. It was a beautiful example of running as an expression both of his spiritual life and his sense of responsibility to his profession. "The last service was the fifth one for me," he said, "but the first one for everyone else who participated. They deserved as good an effort as those who came to the first service got." But if it hadn't been for his discipline of running and the stamina it gave him, they wouldn't have gotten it.

Runners' World (June, 1984) did a special on Sister Marion Irvine, a 55 year old Dominican nun who is principal of Sacred Heart, an inner-city school in San Francisco. She lived a sedentary life until, in her late forties, she was introduced to jogging. In December 1983, by running 2:51:01 at the California International Marathon, she qualified for the Olympic trials. She acknowledges a link between religious and athletic discipline. "I don't draw consciously from my religious training," she says of her capacity for rigor. "But indirectly . . . it makes a decision like whether or not to run in the rain no decision at all. There's no question I'll be out there." The human virtue of discipline involved in religious practices or athletic activities is the very same quality being applied to two different "exercises." For Sr. Marion, the discipline learned in her religious training got her out to run, rain or shine. For someone else, it might work in the other direction: the discipline learned in athletics can make faithfulness to, say, daily reading of Scripture easier.

Sr. Marion also recognizes that running has strong spiritual potential and uses language to describe the experience very close to Glasser's: "In long-distance running, there is a point of harmony between the muscle groups, when the mind is released from any effort of concentration. In that space where the mind is freed, a lot of things can happen. I feel that God put us on earth to be the most complete humans we can be. Running can be a religious thing to do. It provides an opportunity to meditate, and a chance to give glory and praise as well.''

The practice of a spiritual discipline—any concentrated effort to create some inner and outer space in our lives so we may listen with inner ears to life-giving messages—makes us more sensitive to the small, gentle voice of God. The prophet Elijah did not encounter God in the mighty wind or in the earthquake or in the fire, but in the small voice (1 Kings 19:9–13). Through the practice of a spiritual discipline we become more attentive to that small voice and more willing to respond when we hear it. A spiritual discipline is necessary in order to move from a life filled with noisy worries to a life in which there is some free inner space where we can listen to our God and be guided.

Through a spiritual discipline like running or meditating we prevent the world from filling our lives to such an extent that there is no place left to listen. You may never have considered running as a ''spiritual'' discipline, but as this chapter has tried to indicate, there are many reasons why it could be related to as such. If it is good for your body, it's good for your ''soul.'' There is only one, seamless you.

A Peak Experience

The late Abraham Maslow described a peak experience as ''a moment when a person's powers are at their height and he becomes a spontaneous, coordinated, efficient organism functioning with a great flow of power that is so peculiarly effortless that it may become like play.'' *Powers that are coordinated* presume a holistic approach. In our approach to running we have joined practical athletics with spiritual ideas and ideals. In this holistic perspective, running is not just a sport or physical activity so much as a complete expression of ourselves: physical, mental, and spiritual. As such, running contributes to the full and complete development of the person. For this reason all aspects of the self have been integrated into our approach: intuition, sensing, thinking and feeling. Excellence in a particular sport or game is a by-product of this approach, not its main focus. As Glasser's research indicated for those who needed confirmation, only faithfulness to the exercise (discipline) brings one to that point where the mind spins free, where one's experience "peaks" in effortless, coordinated flow.

Eric Little related his running to a larger concern, the life of faith. In "Chariots of Fire," to a crowd of his fans gathered around after a race, he says:

> I want you to compare faith with running in a race. It's hard, requires concentration of will, energy of soul. . . .
> Everyone runs in his or her own way. But where does the power come from to finish the race?
> From within. . . . Commit yourself to the Lord, and he'll see you through to the end.

Chapter 6

Swimming

Gracious God, hear our prayers and bless this water
which gives fruitfulness to the fields,
and refreshment and cleansing to us.
You chose water to show your goodness
when you led your people to freedom
through the Red Sea
and satisfied their thirst in the desert
with water from the rock.
Water was the symbol used by the prophets
to foretell your new covenant with us.
You made the water of baptism holy
by Christ's baptism in the Jordan:
by it you give us a new birth
and renew us in holiness.
May this water remind us of our baptism
and increase our joy.

Rite of Baptism

Plato taught that to be unable to swim is to be uneducated.

Two Scottish scientists, John Durnin and Reginald Passmore, explore the relationship between energy expended through activity and good physical health in their book *Energy, Work and Leisure* (Heineman, London, 1967). They examine a wide variety of physical activities including archery, boxing, cricket, gardening, karate, weight lifting, squash and many others. With regard to swimming they conclude: "This is perhaps the ideal form of exercise."

Why does swimming receive such accolades from ancient philosophers through modern day scientists. Just for starters, let's observe the following: it's clean; you can do it from now to the end of your life without having to worry about excessive strain; the equipment is as minimal as it could be; there's no suffering from pains in the knee, blisters in the feet, or tennis elbow; and the medium of water is refreshing, relaxing, and fun.

Perhaps that's why the latest sports participation study from the A.C. Nielson International Headquarters in Illinois indicates that swimming "remains the single most popular sporting activity." A poll by Long Island's *Newsday* asserts that of 578 randomly selected people, 43% say they swim several times a week in season. Jogging was second with 13%, followed by tennis with 9%. The 1978 Perrier Fitness Survey conducted by the Harris Association found swimming second in popularity only to walking, which just about everybody does anyway. *Sports in America* lists selected sports recommended according to age. Three categories are given for each decade from 5 years of age to 85: "highly recommended," "worth investigating," and "demanding but possible." Swimming appears in the first category, "highly recommended," for the first decade (5–15) and stays there through 75 years old, after which it drops to "worth investigating."

Health specialists don't hesitate to recommend swimming even to senior citizens because the average adult just likes being in the water. It's soothing, it's less strenuous than other exercises and yet, while putting less physical stress on the system than jogging, it is profoundly health-inducing. The blood cells get oxygen, the heart rate lowers and, especially in the case of pools, there's always somebody within ten feet if help is needed.

Swimming also comes highly recommended to leaders and decision-makers because it reduces tension, refreshes the mind as well as the body, and rejuvenates the spirit through the psychic impact of water which, as we will explore later, touches something deep and essential within us. If your job is high-stress, you'll last longer in it if you swim. Swimmers, runners, cross-country skiers share similar outlooks. They seek release from pressures through private exercise and love the feel of their minds and limbs in action.

The various rewards cited in the previous chapter in conjunction with running are also present in swimming: solitude, introspection, achievement, renewal, and joy. I find no contradiction in taking different sports and highlighting the benefits of each one for the simple reason that I am convinced that just one sport won't keep you fit. Fitness is a proportionate combination of strength, flexibility, and endurance. In swimming one probably has the finest alternative to running one can choose.

Varied plans of exercise offer the most advantages for good health because different exercises enhance different body systems. In fair weather months in any given week my activities will encompass running, swimming, biking, and a weight workout. During the winter months, it's skiing, swimming, and weights. I generally exercise six out of seven days a week, choosing one or the other activity, and seldom do it for more than a half an hour. The exceptions would be a full day's ski outing or a bike hike. As we have pointed out earlier, getting one's heartbeat into the target range for fifteen minutes three or four times a week is all that is essentially needed for aerobic fitness. If you're too busy for that amount of exercise on a weekly basis, then you're too busy.

Practical Considerations

EASY TO LEARN   In the minds of many, learning how to swim has been overcomplicated. Somehow we've let ourselves believe that it's a very demanding form of exercise and difficult to learn. What the uninitiated usually do not grasp is that swimming's intensity index can be adjusted all the way from "very slow and leisurely" to "all out," and this at the complete will of the swimmer.

A physical education instructor at the State University of Iowa found in working with twenty beginning women swimmers that in order to pass a 15-minute swimming test the average learning time was five-and-a-half hours distributed in half-hour group lessons. That's the equivalent of about one evening out with your friends. It's no big deal. From there, pick up one of the many "How To Improve Your Swimming" books on the market and read it on your own time.

But most important, keep well in mind Glasser's insight about removing self-criticism. There is a real natural process of learning and performing waiting to be discovered within you. Observe what you do, and then allow your body in a relaxed state and without self-criticism to make its own adjustments. Needless to say, don't try to alter your breathing, your kick, and your head position all at once. Isolate the element you'd like to improve and keep in mind that the improvements you want to make must come only in the name of efficiency, comfort and pleasure. Until you learn to feel your own body's accommodation to moving through water without self-criticism or judgment, you won't achieve whatever changes you're after in the name of efficiency nor will swimming be a pleasurable, relaxing activity.

As for which stroke you should use, use the one that best suits your temperament, that puts you most at ease, and that rests your mind as it exercises your body. Some swimmers stick to a single stroke, others vary their strokes, going from breaststroke to backstroke to crawl to sidestroke. Follow your mood!

THE TIME IT TAKES   In general, one can spend fewer weekly hours at swimming than one needs to spend at other fitness programs because one is exercising more muscles more efficiently. There is a certain psychological advantage to calculating the time swimming takes not only in terms of actual time in the water, but also in terms of all that's involved in the process of arriving and departing. Identify the point at which you stopped whatever else you were doing as the first actual step in your swim outing. The moment you get up from your desk or put away whatever you were working with in the house and reach for your swimbag, the feeling of relaxation begins. Even the process of disrobing and putting on your suit once you have arrived in the locker room can be a symbolic divesting of the stresses and tensions of the day's events. I never liked the pre-swim shower until I started looking upon it as a pre-purification ritual, a rinsing off of the very feeling of heaviness that may result from the tasks and challenges of the day. Though my body is usually ready for exercise when I arrive, my head usually has a little catching-up to do, and the pre-swim shower brings it along quickly, washing out thoughts and concerns that are still trailing behind back at the office. The shower is an initial relaxant that the swim will extend and expand.

The same approach holds for after the swim. Instead of climbing out of the pool with your heart racing and going directly into the showers after your last lap, allow yourself some cooldown time by just floating, or sitting in the water on the steps in the shallow end, or by doing a gentle side- or backstroke. "Cooldown" is not necessary in swimming as in other sports because the body temperature which ordinarily rises with exercise has been prevented from rising by the coolness of the water. Still, taking a few minutes to allow the pulse rate to return to normal and to simply enjoy the pleasurable medium of the water leaves one feeling more relaxed and calm.

What yet remains is all part of the process, too: showering, shampooing, toweling down—each contributes in its own way to the process of renewal. By the time you put your clothes back on again, you've got a very different feeling than the one with which you arrived. The transforming effect of swimming is what causes some to say that it's the part of their lives that makes the rest of their lives run smoothly. Or, as one fellow put it: "I'd be crazy not to do regularly anything that makes me feel this good." In short, the rewards are worth the effort of doing some jockeying around with your family's schedule or your office schedule to break away when the pool is available. Harvey S. Wiener, in his excellent book *Total Swimming* (Simon and Schuster, 1980), offers some practical suggestions:

1. Hire a babysitter for an hour or two during the day or evening. If the sitter stays while the child sleeps, you won't miss any time with your baby. And in this way, husband and wife can swim together. You might even pack up sitter and child. Let them come to the pool along with you.

2. Take turns with your spouse. One of you babysits one night, the other another night.

3. Take turns with neighbors. Watch their kids during one part of the day; give them yours at a time when you want to swim.

4. Check with the pool facility itself. Many exercise centers, especially the private clubs, offer babysitting services while parents are exercising. At a large recreation center you can often sign up a child for some planned activity (like arts and crafts, dance, drawing, skating) while you're swimming.

5. Swim between your car pooling assignments. Harriet Clark in Detroit drops the boys off at little league practice, swims while they're playing, and then returns refreshed and invigorated to pick up her brood. Just how much are you pressed for time? (p. 116)

Water as Symbol

Before returning to school for my final year of theology studies, I decided to take several days at summer's end and go on a solo backpack trip in the mountains. It had been an intensive summer and I felt in need of the tonic of the outdoors and the wide open mountain spaces. It was the first time I had ventured out alone, but in light of several previous backpacking experiences, I felt comfortable doing so.

The first night, I camped in a valley at the foot of the mountain and awoke in the early morning light to find myself surrounded by a half dozen grazing deer. After they departed, I broke camp and prepared myself for the first day's climb. My map indicated that there were three or four springs along the way at regular intervals. Wanting to carry only the weight that was absolutely necessary, I used most of the water in my canteen for breakfast preparations and cleanup.

The first few hours' climb in the cool of the morning passed quickly and enjoyably. Nonetheless, I looked forward to my arrival at the first spring indicated on my map. My disappointment was real but it evoked no alarm within me when I discovered the first spring was dry. I continued to climb, and so did the sun. By early afternoon I was sweating freely and experiencing considerable thirst. The second spring was not far away.

When I arrived at that place on the trail where there should have been a spring, only moisture on the rocks indicated the place where earlier in the summer water had freely flowed. I began to feel angry. At my own stupidity for having unnecessarily used my water supply. At the mountain and my map for promising, but not delivering. This time I not only wanted to drink, but knew I *needed* to drink. The prospect of several more hours' climb in the hot sun was not a favorable one.

Gauging the distance on my map to the next spring, I set off again, hovering between skepticism and hope. It was early evening by the time I arrived, and dusk was beginning to fall. This water-source, too, was barren. While in my head I knew that a person can survive a long time without water, viscerally I felt distressed and in trouble. The food I was carrying was in powder or freeze-dried form and also depended upon water to bring it to life.

I was by now at the top of the first crest and decided to use the rest of the remaining light to seek out a suitable place for sleeping. Darkness came quickly and the wind in the cedar trees played tricks with my ears, creating illusions of a trickling stream. At one point, convinced that wish-fulfillment was playing havoc with my hearing, I followed the sound through the darkness with more than a little desperation. When my steps led me to a small running stream in the rocks, I fell on my knees and bathed my face in the cool current.

Water has never been the same for me since.

Later that night, I took a small journal from my backpack and, sitting in front of the fire, under the stars, tried to capture the experience:

Angry.
At the mountain
    for its miles being longer than they should

for its springs being dry
for its disappearing trails
for its gila monster crest
Angry.
Darkness free-falls like a paratrooper with stuck chute.
No water
for my lynched throat
and squeeze-dried body.
Ears are on tip-toe—
for the sound of a breeze trickling
or spring whispering—
Wanting illusion even.
Listen—
that lisp in the forest's speech—
Listen:
(a rush of hope
gives breathless pause
to shrouding night)
Listen.
Yes!
Spring!
I am springing!
Unsprung!
Trickling earth-blood
Melted ice-water
Snow-man's sweat
raining on my tongue
cracked like baked unraked soil.
Saving water
to wash in
to refresh with
Rescuing from fear and brooding.
O life-giving Spirit
hovering over the waters
and creating order out of chaos
O thirst-quenching Savior

walking on water
and dispelling anxiety with your presence
O covenanting-Father
giving us in flood
an image of new birth:
I praise you for this water
this cleansing and refreshment
this supporting strength
this saving sign of your love and care
That touches us with a power and endurance beyond our fragile
lives.

Prior to that experience, I had largely taken for granted the water that flows forth abundantly from our spigots and shower-heads and hoses. After that experience, water has been sacred to the point where even dripping spigots that waste it find me moving to tighten them or change the washer. I don't want to overstress the symbolic qualities of water—regeneration, renewal, rebirth—but I do want to touch upon what it represents to the mind and emotions by virtue of our primordial relatedness to water.

Harvey Wiener reflects on our liquid beginnings by noting how ocean water alone covers two-thirds of the earth's surface. It is not only abundant, but incredibly varied: cold makes it solid in snow or ice; heat vaporizes it into steam. It is essential in nutrition and vital in industry as a catalyst and solvent. Water figures critically in transportation, disposal, cleansing, power, and cooling.

Evolutionary theory today points to beginnings in the sea, early life forms moving from saline environments to fresh water and land only after five hundred million years. Biologically, then, humanity in a sense owes itself to water and swimming, for the human animal took shape through time and evolution from those forms that first swam about. "And after one champion swimmer sperm fertilizes an egg," Weiner writes, "each one of us growing in the womb seems to pass through the stages through which the whole human species developed since time's beginnings. So at one time in everyone's life he or she is a swimmer of sorts. With gill arches and yolk sacs in those early prenatal days, we have the same primitive features as fish.'' The amniotic sac inside of which a human being takes shape and grows is called an ''intrauterine swimming pool'' by Dr. Claes Wirsen, author of *A Child Is Born.*

We may have trouble now in taking the plunge into water when we are standing dry on the shore of a lake or the edge of a pool, but then it was the other way around. The breaking of the amniotic sac and the entry into air was such a sudden environmental change that it constituted a large part of our birth trauma. It is not uncommon for obstetricians to insist that the newborn be bathed immediately in warm water to calm the shock. The environment of water offers the comfort of continuity with the child's earliest phase of development and reduces the shock of entry into the world of air.

We shouldn't be surprised, then, to hear someone remark, ''I love swimming! My time in the pool is the peace and the calm of the womb.'' It's a return, in a symbolic sense, to our amniotic state. Says Wiener, ''Swimming as a sport returns us to a familiar medium of harmony, perhaps to an unconscious association with our amniotic voyage. Further, the water through which we move duplicates the inner makeup of the human organism; all our tissues are immersed in and composed of fluid. And the rhythmic motions of the water have resonances with bodily processes.''

Against the backdrop of those reflections, a statement such as ''When I swim I feel as if my life is beginning again'' makes a lot of sense. To be sure, water for the swimmer is simply a soothing environment in which he or she can exercise comfortably. And yet the symbolic features are fascinating. When you immerse yourself in water you are touching your own origins. The water that swirls about you represents nature and religion and birth and sex and survival.

Psychological Benefits

Prior to the last couple of years, I swam only infrequently. To be sure, being in the water was always a fun and refreshing experience, but swimming *as* swimming was never one of my favorite forms of activity. I would not go out of my way to find a pool. The occasional lake on a hot summer's day sufficed.

The growth of my appreciation for swimming as a sport is related to an increase of responsibility and pressure in my work. Because of its ability to ease the mind, release daily tensions and leave me feeling fresh and renewed, swimming has had a meteoric rise in my choice of activity. If, by the time I get to my locker, I still don't have a clear preference as to what I want to do that day—swimming, running, weights—I will inevitably reach for my swim trunks. Swimming never misses. I *always* feel better after a swim.

With a minimum of equipment, preparation, and travel time, swimming creates an inner-state of harmony and well-being that feels almost magical. I used to dismiss reflections such as those made on the previous pages as "romantic" and "poetic." But now the transformation that takes place within me through 15 minutes in the pool is so real that I am forced to conclude that the water medium touches something deep and primordial.

A holistic approach to life leaves no doubt about the direct relationship between work performance, physical fitness and emotional well-being. It is those who come up short on the last two whose marks are highest in the columns of absenteeism, sickness, diminished productivity, and anxiety. Stress management has become a favorite subject of corporation counseling. Exercise is always a key element in any dealing-with-stress strategy. If the job's a hot seat, those who swim will be able to sit on it longer without getting burned.

The combination of total immersion, cleansing, rhythmic breathing, a sense of play, and the sheer pleasurable feel of water on the skin provides swimming with certain tranquilizing properties. The vexation of our daily lives dissolves like an alka-seltzer tablet dropped in—you guessed it—water! The state of post-swim relaxation endures for hours, and new energy is released to enable problems to be dealt with decisively but without frenzy, nervousness or strain.

I've noticed, too, that the water has a mysterious effect upon the mental processes. If I'm experiencing brain-fatigue and can no longer deal with numbers or words or concepts, shifting the area of stress from mental to physical renews the faculties of perception and creativity. The unfinished task doesn't seem nearly as difficult after the swim.

The past few months have severely tested the hardiness of my social support systems and the reliability of my safety-valve mechanisms. Within the space of a few short months, the senior, founding partner of the Ecumenical Centre retired, an assistant director in his early forties died of cancer, another assistant was hospitalized with phlebitis, the director of our library changed jobs, and a secretary left for personal reasons. In a brief lapse of time, our normal working staff of 12 fell to six. Demand for services was higher than ever, but supply lower than ever. We cut back on our commitments where feasible, but certain annual contracts, magazine publishing dates, and the like required doing the best we could under the circumstances. Deadline followed deadline, road-trip followed road-trip, and there have been days when the stress felt like a hard fist in the middle of my chest.

Presently, we are in the middle of a third non-stop month, but the pressure is easing and we are managing to replace needed personnel as we go along. During the past week, in spite of getting to bed early, I began to notice a foreign, early-afternoon fatigue. I named it depression, the kind that comes from personal loss, overwork, or both. Leaving the projects and dossiers behind, I headed for the silence and woods enveloping the House of Prayer at the foot of Mount St. Hilaire in the Eastern Townships of Quebec. While there, with the detached perspective that distance and a reflective atmosphere offer, I looked at the crazy pace of the last months. Despite our best efforts to order our lives sanely, there are certain periods where unexpected developments explode our carefully laid plans and threaten to override all systems of checks and balances. One of my reactions was astonishment that the prolonged level of stress had not resulted in some psychosomatic symptom like a cold or sore throat. I am convinced that the answer lies in the daily exercise and meditation to which I cling firmly.

Depression is both physical and mental, and exercise is one guarantee against it. The relaxation and renewal that swimming provides found me choosing it over other forms of exercise during this very taxing stretch. I credit it in a special way for the balanced temperament and good health of the past months. At a time when I have needed something reliable but simple, this activity, with its definite and unchangeable boundaries, its medium controlled for purity and temperature, has been the answer. If "stay cool" was the prescription, swimming was the formula.

Just about anyone who has ever spent some time in a pool and emerged from a hot shower afterwards will describe the feeling-state in the same word: relaxed. One's whole makeup, physical and mental, feels harmonized. For many, swimming has been a step toward that quality or style of life that we have earlier described as leisure. Some see it as something they do for themselves, alone, away from their job, their friends, the world. Partly by virtue of the action itself (swimming is the only activity one has to do alone), partly because of the solitude, there comes a freedom and an encounter with the inner self.

Others give up swimming for that very reason, saying they "can't stand being in their heads so long." But one doesn't have to *think*. The elements of repetition and familiarity in performing the strokes, especially when coupled with deep rhythmic breathing, open up the altered state of consciousness described earlier in running and skiing. Glasser spoke of the "spinning free" experience of runners. Here, a similar expression is even more apropos, "floating free," in the cool blue peace.

There are certain things that make mental spinning or floating free easier in swimming than in other physical activities. The mental processes are directed inward because one's senses, normally dependent upon the outside world for information, are in a state of altered perception. With or without goggles, water density makes visual images different. Eyes, ears, nose, mouth, and hands become limited receptors in the water. Consequently, the mind, receiving less, unusual, and muted sensory data, is freed to focus upon inner states. The reliable, unchanging, predictable environment of a pool gives further permission to "let go" on a tour of the mental landscape, allowing thoughts and feelings free play.

It is precisely here, close to self, moving peacefully through one's environment with an attitude of trust and security, that experiences which could justly be described as "spiritual" occur. There is a slipping from conscious mental activity and a simple sense of awareness of one's inner self, one's spirit, which is closely akin to the experience of meditation in which there is an express effort to shut down normal mental processes and to simply "be" on another, deeper, level. This state of thoughtlessness is induced by repetition over distance. The sense of release may come after 15 or 25 laps, depending on one's mental and physical makeup. At times my first 10 laps are mental complaint. "I'm going to stop *now* and just go sit in the sauna." Then as my muscles get looser and a sense of fluidity comes, there is a slipping over into a marvelous experience of harmony of *being*. Sometimes it doesn't come at all and the feeling of tiredness with which I began does not go away. There's no way to predict it. But there's no mistaking it when it happens.

The use of mantra in meditation is, in a sense, paralleled by either concentration on one's breathing (I know one Orthodox priest who prays the Jesus prayer) or counting laps; in either case, the concentration on one or the other serves to suspend thought, which contributes to the higher state of relaxation, to the experience of "floating free." There is a sense of rhythmic, almost effortless energy flow, a sense of ease and vitality.

Arrival at this psychic space is not surprising when one looks at the factors involved in swimming over-against the conditions invariably cited for meditation: a quiet environment; deep, regular breathing; suspension of normal thought processes; and an open, "let it happen" state of mind. Add the soothing and sensual medium of water, Glasser's advice about no negative self-criticism, and there is no way this experience can be anything other than deeply relaxing, if not mildly euphoric. While repetitive physical activities do allow us to transcend the normal boundaries of our restrictive consciousness, for many swimmers the special secret of euphoria is simply *water* and its mysterious capacity to invite psychological elation. Nonetheless, despite the magic of water, I would suggest that one's degree of psychological elation depends on how long one swims and how one uses one's mind in the process. As Glasser discovered with runners, one can't realize the extraordinary results in body and mind unless one swims actively, often, and for certain minimal periods of time.

Granted, if you're a beginner, you will have to pay attention to specific actions in the water to improve your efficiency and build up your stamina to a point where you can swim for 15–20 minutes easefully. But even in the beginning stages, don't fret so much about mechanics that you are not able to *enjoy* just being in the water. Self-criticism evokes feelings of discouragement and steals away important psychological advantages. Just use all the sensory receptors with which you're endowed to enjoy the experience. *Feel* the coolness of the water on your skin. *Listen* to the rhythmic sound of your breathing. *Look* at the soft quality of filtered light. *Smell* the salt-sea air. Before long, what was once tedious will be a major contributor to your ever-expanding experience of life called wellness.

Physical Benefits

The dangers of overstress are minimal in the controlled environment of a pool. The activity is by nature self-limited, i.e. one can't go any faster or longer than one's lungs or heart will permit. This is one of the reasons why swimming is ideal for all ages: it's easy to control output. The body's own built-in mechanisms will prevent any excess. Even if some years have slipped by with no regular pattern of physical exercise, one can still pick up at some level and work up several notches. Since it may have taken lots of years to get out of shape, go slowly in getting back into it. Slowly, but regularly.

Regular exercise becomes more important with the march of time. Some observers of the trends in modern society criticize the present fitness movement by saying that it represents a subconscious denial of our mortality and finitude. Personally, I do the best I can to accept that I'm getting older and will eventually die, but what bothers me is that so many of us seem to feel and act old *before* our time. Jan and Lloyd Percival and Joe Taylor say in their *Complete Guide to Total Fitness* (Prentice-Hall of Canada, 1977, p. 23) that "five out of six North Americans are older physiologically than they are chronologically. What's the point of celebrating a 30th birthday, for example, if our muscles and heart and lungs say we're 40?" While we *are* getting older, we don't have to *feel* older than we are! Gerontologists say that the average person's productive adult life can be extended past the present average by some 20 percent through regular physical activity of the proper type. That means that what an individual can do in his or her 50's, he or she should be able to do at 70.

The *New York Times Magazine,* in an article entitled "Athletes: Older But Fitter" (October 20, 1984, pp. 90–102), challenged some traditional concepts with new research findings.

The traditional concept has been that, from about 30 on, "age costs you a loss in endurance of at least 1 percent a year," says David L. Costill, director of the Human Performance Laboratory, a sports research facility at Ball State University, in Muncie, Ind. "But that level of degradation is because of inactivity. People just naturally say, 'Oh, you're getting older, so you're losing your endurance.' What you are really doing is becoming less active."

According to Costill, studies have shown that "for those top-quality athletes who maintain a rigorous training schedule over the years, the loss of endurance tends to be tiny fractions of a percentage point."

For many years these conditions were thought to be the inevitable, irreversible results of the passage of time. But according to Everett L. Smith, director of the Biogerontology Laboratory in the University of Wisconsin's department of preventive medicine, 50 percent of the decline in each of these functions is a result of "disuse atrophy," or neglect, and his studies indicate that the loss from disuse can be regained through exercise.

"Age is not a limiting factor to increasing fitness," Smith says. "It is possible, for instance, to regain up to 60 percent of the loss of cardiovascular function with regular exercise."

At the Biogerontology Laboratory, Smith and his staff have tested women from 35 to 65 in exercise programs and found that "there is virtually a straight line in improvement; the 65-year-olds show the same ratio of improvement as the 35-year-olds."

Dr. Zohman of Montefiore says, "A lot of what we have thought of as disease, or the onset of disease, in older people—breathlessness, multiple aches and pains, a quickness to exhaustion—is really deconditioning."

Costill points out that studies indicate younger athletes fall out of shape every bit as quickly as older ones: "We kept track of guys on the Ball State swimming team who put in 10,000 meters in the pool every day during the season. Once the season ends, some of them don't do anything more strenuous than lift a beer bottle. Within two months they've lost it. They're totally out of shape.'' Deterioration ''takes about eight weeks,'' then ''they're only slightly better than any ordinary sedentary individual their age.''

''A lot of people are attracted to a sport initially because of the health aspect,'' says Hal Higdon. ''They've had the first of their midlife crises and are coming to grips with mortality. They realize they're out of shape and need to do something about it.

''But once they've been doing it for six or eight weeks and they get their cardiovascular systems responding and the soreness is past, then they start to realize the other pleasures to be had.''

Swimming is not only pleasurable but will get one's heart and lungs in excellent aerobic condition. In the Appendix at the back, pulse-rate monitoring is discussed. The chart cited there should be slightly adjusted for swimmers who want to figure the best pulse rates for their age. Desirable heart rates for swimmers are lower than for runners and cross-country skiers. First of all, as soon as you get into the cool water of a pool, the heart rate falls and you're at a lower rate to begin with. Secondly, your skin, surrounded by that water, needs less blood supply for cooling than would be the case in running; the water helps your body to release the heat generated in swimming. This means that the circulatory system can deliver oxygen more efficiently to the exercising muscles. Finally, the prone body position in the water enables blood to flow more easily back to the heart, which also holds the pulse rate down.

Consequently, training levels of heart beat rate will be lower in swimming than in other activities. The following chart adjusts the maximum heart beat rate for swimmers in column B and then gives the desirable exercise or training rate in column C. There are slight variations in column A as one progresses in age with the chart cited in the Appendix, but not enough to be significant.

By getting the pulse up to the desired training rate for the duration of a 15 minute swim, the heart is strengthened so that it works more efficiently when it is at rest. As one becomes a better

MAXIMUM PULSE RATES: A COMPARISON

Age	A	B	C
	MPRs (For running and other land activities)	Adjusted MPRs (For swimmers)	Swimmers' Training Rate
20	200	187	131
25	195	182	128
28	192	179	125
30	190	177	124
32	188	175	123
35	185	172	121
38	182	169	118
40	180	167	117
42	178	166	116
45	175	162	114
48	172	159	112
50	170	157	110
52	168	155	109
55	165	152	107
58	162	149	104
60	160	147	103
62	156	145	102
65	155	142	100
68	152	139	98
70	150	137	96
72	148	135	95
75	145	132	93
78	142	129	91
80	140	127	89

Total Swimming Harvey S. Wiener p. 226, 1980, Simon & Schuster

swimmer, one will have to swim more intensively to achieve the training pulse rate. But as long as one monitors the heart beat and keeps it around 70–80 percent of the maximum heart beat rate for one's age, there is no reason to fear over-exercising.

Swimming is great for muscle tone as well, for just about every muscle in the body is involved. Although swimming and running both work the heart satisfactorily, swimming has the added advantage of developing musculature above the waist. Runner's upper bodies tend to thin out when their sport is not coupled with another involving vigorous upper body activity. It's the combined effort of cardio-respiratory and muscle systems in cross-country skiing that makes it the king of aerobic exercises.

For those who suffer from chronic back pain, swimming is tops because the water bears most of the weight of the body. Because of its nature as an anti-gravity sport, swimming is unsurpassed for the handicapped or for people recovering from an illness. Patients who choose water sports for therapy show marked gains in confidence, self-image and renewal of mental stamina as well as physical.

Covert Bailey, however, does not recommend swimming for people who are overfat and who wish to lose weight. Body fat tests done in water immersion programs indicate that there is no reduction in fat when a person embarks on a swimming program. In contrast to the runner's body, which will shed as much weight as possible, "the swimmer's body tends to conserve its fat in order to provide warmth and buoyancy during the exercise. Every sea-living mammal has made a similar adaption. . . . In other words, swimming is a great aerobic program, but you'd better add some other exercises to your program if you're overfat" (*Fit or Fat?* pp. 40–41).

As has been maintained all along, total fitness is not to be found with any one single activity.

To relocate this discussion of swimming in the overall context of wellness, we would have to go a step farther and say that athletic activities are just one contributing factor to "our ever-expanding experience of purposeful and pleasurable living."

In its own unique way, swimming certainly nurtures freedom of spirit, enables us to transcend the dimensions of economic and social necessity, heightens our experience of the quality of life, and yields sense and style to our way of living.

This experience of leisure is in direct relation to that incarnationalist, creation-centered spirituality which identifies more and fuller life as both our human and our spiritual aim.

Chapter 7

Skiing

Preface for Winter

We give you thanks, O Lord, for times and seasons
We give you thanks, O Lord, for times and seasons
and now for winter nights
when stars shine coldly bright
and dust is turned to diamonds underfoot.
For winter days
when trees are stronger than the icy death
and hold in blackened limbs
the promise of the resurrection.
For opposites be praised: for heat and cold,
for stillness and the snow
that sculptures every house and tree, and falls
like some great absolution
to heal the wounded earth.

We give you thanks for him
whose birth we celebrate in winter
so all may know, may wildly know,
that love is stronger than the coldest flesh
and mercy blankets all the land
more surely than the snow.
We give you thanks for him
who makes more than children joyful
and does not cheat our laughter in the end.

Joyous Lord,
beyond imagining but not beyond desire,
we give you glory and our song of praise.

Joseph Thomas Nolan

Those of us who work in ecumenism are not into sheep-stealing; rather, we are interested in gathering the flocks together into one fold. We respect the riches of each particular tradition or Church, but encourage the common search for agreement in faith on divisive issues which will enable all to come together in a real unity wherein the treasures of each mutually shared will make all richer. Consequently, we do not look kindly upon proselytizing.

However, there is one area of my life in which I break all my own rules. When it comes to cross-country skiing, I am an absolutely shameless proselytizer. When the subject is even casually mentioned to me, if within five minutes I have not been able to evoke in the other at least the desire to try it, I consider myself to have miserably failed to preach the word effectively enough. I will do my best to control this blessed urge in these reflections on skiing and to give equal time to downhill skiing, of which I am also very fond.

If, as Glasser claimed, running is our most ancient survival mechanism and a good run reactivates the ancient neural program, skiing was probably the form running took in certain northern climes. Did you ever try running in hip deep snow? It doesn't work very well. But clamp flat strips of smooth wood on your feet and, well, that's another story. Skiing, all skiing, evolved from the utilitarian necessity of wintertime travel. Nobody knows how old skiing was when a pictograph of a skier was hewn on a rock wall in arctic Norway some 4,500 years ago. Skiing was already more than 4,000 years old when in 1674 Johan Scheffer related his travels among the Lapps of northern Europe, describing their cross-country skiing in Latin and wood cuts.

Cross-country skiing on this continent is an anachronism, the oldest yet newest and now-fastest growing winter sport. There's something in it for everyone. It can be as totally private as a lone skier on a mountain plateau or as sociable as a race where sometimes thousands ski together. One can ski cross-country in terrain as benign as a snow-covered city park or golf course, or in the heart of the most rugged mountain ranges of the world. It can be done in prepared, manicured tracks, made for rhythm and speed, or in untracked snows wherever they may lie. Cross-country skiing can be as flashy or as rustic as suits individual skier preference. It knows no limits of age, sex, income, or physical ability.

As Michael Brady recounts in *The Complete Ski Cross-Country* (The Dial Press, 1982) skiing as a leisure activity spread rapidly through the Alps of Europe, in Switzerland, Austria, Italy, France, and Germany. Unlike the major mountain chains of North America, the Alps are relatively populated, with villages, towns, and even cities in the valleys below the peaks. Many who lived in the rugged Alpine terrain took up skiing. The sport was to climb up, or sometimes take a train up, to a higher village, and whiz down. The appeal was the unidirectional thrill. Then, as more and more people took up the sport, devices were built to haul them uphill so they could pack more downhill runs into a day of skiing.

Lifts were also built in North America, as immigrants and returning tourists brought Alpine skiing from Europe. The sport evolved; more lifts and ski areas were built. The excitement of the downhill plunge on skis caught on, especially in the large cities of the Eastern part of the continent. Regular ski trains to the snow became part of the wintertime recreation scene by the late 1930's. Then, after World War II, the sport of skiing downhill grew so rapidly that it eclipsed the parent sport of what is now known as cross-country skiing. The equipment for the former was steadily refined for downhill skiing performance and ease. And because machines did the uphill work, that unidirectional thrill could be had even more often and more easily. In the public consciousness, the sport became just "skiing."

So when the original form of skiing reappeared, it was viewed as a totally different sport by the skiing community and came to be termed cross-country or Nordic skiing to differentiate it from downhill or Alpine skiing. In Scandinavia, for example, where the original meanings have been retained, if you want to look up the results of an Alpine slalom ski race in a Norwegian newspaper, you don't look under "ski," because that's where you find the results of cross-country ski races. You look under *"Alpine."*

As cross-country skiing enters the second decade of its renaissance, many downhill skiers have discovered the joys of cross-country, and many cross-country skiers have taken up Alpine skiing as a second sport. Surveys have shown that at least a quarter of the skiers in each group practice the other sport. I am one of those, and I speak willingly of the joys of both.

Cross-country is easier to learn, more accessible, cheaper (and hence more family oriented), safer, quieter, and a more total-body form of exercise. While both are exhilarating, downhill clearly has more high-level thrills. While downhill tends to show one the peaks of mountains and cross-country the forests below, both offer a rich visual experience. Downhill seems to be the clear preference for those in the 13–22 age range seemingly because it's "less work" and more sociable, e.g. the opportunity to visit with people on the lifts, around the fireplace between runs, and, of course, après ski.

While downhill skiing requires large hills or mountains, cities are fast discovering how to use their parks to good advantage for cross-country skiers. When it's Saturday in New York City and the crowds are worse than cockroaches in a West Side high rise, New Yorkers are learning to grab their peanut butter bars from a corner health-food store and hail a cab for Central Park where Belvedere Castle looms up like a wintry gothic fantasy. The blue-haired ladies clutching Gucci bags may throw some curious looks, but that's a small price to pay for a couple of precious hours removed from the electric high wires of city life.

Like New York, the snow in Chicago is wholly unpredictable. It can be depressingly whimpy, or it can fall with sufficient fury to paralyze the city for a week. Cross-country enthusiasts need, in addition to their skiing skills, the patience of a Zen master to endure the shut-in-days before winter's snow falls. When it arrives, a satisfying set of tracks can be laid down in any of the parks along the city's 23 miles of Lake Michigan shoreline. Though the city crowds in one side of the parks, there is always the lake on the other, providing visual relief and a sense of up-country openness. A late-season storm can usually be relied upon to blanket the parks with a foot of fresh powder, and for skiers, in those few brief shining moments all the city's climatic sins are suddenly forgiven.

Minnesotans are simply spoiled, with 513 parks between Minneapolis and St. Paul alone and ski trails to satisfy beginners and experts alike. Minnesota, like Toronto, Ontario, has factored in a new element of interest to the cross-country experience: ski-touring through the zoo. Toronto's zoo is built on a cageless-compound design and an afternoon on skis, though just a subway or bus ride from home, is like being on a winter safari. And as for Montreal, well, if you know of another city in the world that has 65 kilometers of groomed trails right within the city, let me know, because I haven't heard of it. You can practically step off the subway, clamp on your skis, and disappear into any one of five different wooded parks.

For the sake of the exercise, so to speak, let's approach the subject of skiing in terms of the characteristics of leisure. To avoid categorical overlap, I will combine the characteristics of "nurtures freedom of spirit" with "enables one to transcend the dimensions of economic and social necessity and to participate in experiences that are more qualitatively satisfying'' into one heading. Further, I think we can combine ''yielding sense and style to one's way of living'' with ''enables discovery of grace and peace in one's daily walk'' because they both are in close relationship to each other. And finally, I will allow ''heightening one's experience of the quality of life'' to stand alone. Let us begin with this last characteristic of a leisure activity.

Does it heighten my experience of the quality of life?

A friend, recently returned from a downhill ski vacation in Colorado, penned me a letter while still in the afterglow. A lyrical excerpt provides an enthusiastic response to the question: does skiing heighten my experience of the quality of life?

> Skiing is an exhilaration matched by few other sports I have tried. The rush of brisk, cold air against my face as I glide freely down a slope . . . the spray of sparkling snow around me . . . the thrill of seeming to fly down a mountain mixed with the challenge of form, control and grace . . . the call upon my physical prowess in intimate face-off with the glory of nature . . . soaking up sunlight brilliantly reflected off crystals of snow . . . screaming through mounds of white powder . . . dancing with the stars through silent, frosted blue-green pines: all these glories speak to me of the incomparable love of the Creator who gives these gifts without condition. Sharpening my sensitivities, my awareness, increasing my capacity to receive this gift gives me a growing awareness of God, not just in evergreens and rosy cheeks but in many other everyday aspects of his creation. Responding to this Presence sensed in everyday experiences is a little bit of worship, each moment, each day.

I couldn't agree more. About a week after my friend came back from Colorado, I went to Alberta to give some conferences and took my skis along for some play in the Rockies at Banff and

Lake Louise. So compelling is the sheer natural beauty that it's the only place I've skied in North America where, during my whole first day on the mountain, the act of skiing itself felt like a distraction. Even Europeans who ski at these two stations readily confess that the Canadian Rockies, with their dramatic rise and sharp definition, can hold their own with the Alps for sheer visual stimulation. On one occasion, I took a lift up to the very peak and crossed over the top, gliding down into a back bowl. Within seconds I discovered myself completely alone in a vast expanse of space, with the jagged peaks towering above me, no other skier in sight and not a sound to be heard. I stood transfixed for a long while. The Scriptures use the word "theophany" for such moments when the divine is experienced breaking through and transfiguring natural events with a sense of the sacred. When I finally pushed off with my poles, I did so slowly and deliberately, with a sense of one touched by the Holy and visited with awe. Even now, months later, I can recall that experience and those feelings with astonishing clarity. I have no other word for it than mystical—a level of experience to which I am convinced we are all called. It is primarily a question of refining our inner and outer senses to the presence of the Holy, daily in our midst.

Does it free my spirit and enable me to transcend social and economic necessities?

Timothy Gallway and Bob Kriegel, in their book *Inner Skiing*, (Random House, 1977), hold up a mirror in which many skiers find their images reflected: longing to spend a few days in the mountains away from the cement, fumes, and frantic rush, one arrives after a five-hour drive exhausted. Undaunted, one awakes at dawn, gulps down breakfast and rushes to the mountain, tense and complaining about the long lift lines.

Their book is an invitation to simply feel the exhilaration of one's body in motion, to observe the beauty of one's surroundings, and to question whether more is necessarily better, whether in ski runs or possessions. For the pleasure of skiing lies in being totally involved, in the way one feels when the body is in motion, whether in the sense of natural rhythm and flow in parallel turns gracefully executed or in the kick'n glide of a cross-country straight-away. The goal is a feeling of harmony both with ourselves and with our environment. As is always the case with genuine play, the prize is in the experience itself. Skiing so experienced gives way to inner-exaltation and is truly re-creation, lifting our spirits from the mire of concerns that otherwise weigh us down.

Play only gives this freedom of spirit as long as it remains truly play. Our achievement orientation may be so strong that we turn every play into a feat of grim performance. Anxious competition may take over and make relaxation impossible. Thus, the tennis ranch becomes another place of work where we must compulsively prove our worth. Mountain travel deteriorates into a struggle against time and fellow travelers, an endurance test that blinds us to the breath-taking vistas all around. If we lose our capacity for play, we also lose our capacity for contemplation, for openness to those moments of theophany, for "useless" presence to the divine.

The concentration of children at play offers a beautiful example of what concentration really is: the child's mind is relaxed but totally engaged. There is no thinking about the activity—just pure experiencing. Because one's ability to enjoy is usually in direct proportion to one's ability to concentrate, the element of concentration is of crucial importance. Whatever totally absorbs us is enjoyable whether it be a good book, a television program, working in the garden, or skiing. Relaxed concentration is the key to genuine leisure, to freedom of spirit, to the freedom which allows us to transcend the concerns in which we are much invested and which we sometimes experience as a burden; that freedom which is a foretaste of eternity rather than a particle of time. To the extent one loses one's ability to be absorbed, to concentrate in a relaxed manner, one becomes powerless to enjoy, to experience with intensity and passion, to love.

The very quality of our daily experience of living depends on the development of these master skills: concentration and awareness. We have all spent time in the presence of people who seem incapable of bringing their attention to settle upon any point of interest for more than a few moments. Time with them is generally not satisfying because it lacks focus. The quality of one's concentration can make the difference between a life that is satisfying and fulfilled and one that is distracted searching. Two cross-country skiers can take the same run through a pine forest freshly laid with a soft cloth of intricate white lace and have an entirely different experience—one with head up reveling in the glories of creation, the other with head down counting the kilometers and looking at a wristwatch gauging how much longer until he can eat his peanut butter and jelly sandwich. The difference in their perceptions lies in the quality of their attention.

In downhill skiing, skiing with beautiful form doesn't automatically lead to an experience that is pleasurable and enjoyable, just as skiing poorly does not have to be equated with an unhappy day. What makes the difference is the ability of the skier to appreciate the totality of the experience itself. The quality of our experiencing is up to us; value lies within and flows from the attitudes and convictions which condition our view of the world and our place within it. One's spirituality is of immense importance because it shapes our response to everything that is going on and thus has the power to change the quality of the entire range of one's experience.

Gallway and Kriegel concur:

> Skiers and non-skiers alike tend to assume that the quality of their experience is the result of what is happening to them, so we put too much energy into changing externals. We look for better ski tips, better jobs, better homes, better husbands and

wives. Although we can alter our lives by changing our environment, most significant changes occur when we find effective ways to change our inner landscape, because that is the environment that we will always have with us. (p. 136)

The goal of wellness is an ever expanding experience of pleasurable and purposeful living motivated by spiritual values and religious beliefs. Since experiencing is our fundamental activity, and since the quality of our lives depends on the quality of our experience, we will look more closely at the critical factor in the process of experiencing: our ability to be *aware*.

I suggest that skiing, by its very nature as an activity which requires a fairly high degree of focused concentration, helps one develop this quality of awareness which is all-important for the larger game of life. One often hears skiers remark: "The only place I succeed in putting everything out of my mind is on the skihill." That is due, I think, to two factors: the exhilarating nature of the sport itself, and the simple fact that if one does not pay close attention to what one is doing, one will end up in short order either wrapped around a tree or tangled in the arms and legs of another skier.

The brief introduction to the principles of Zen that we had in the few excerpts from *Zen in the Art of Archery* in Chapter Four need to be recalled here. The books *Inner Skiing* and *Inner Tennis* are, in fact, based on the principle of Zen. The reasoning is straightforward: when the mind is in a state of alertness, the body is poised and ready to respond to any situation. One's feeling for one's skis and one's sensitivity to the changes in terrain are heightened.

For the last two years I have participated in the granddaddy of all ski marathons in North America and the longest in the world, the Canadian Ski Marathon, which runs from Lachute in Québec to Ottawa in Ontario the second weekend of February each year. It is an unforgettable two-day outdoor experience on a spectacular trail covering 160 km (100 miles) along rivers, across lakes, through Indian reservations and over mountains. There are two categories of participation: *coureur de bois,* for those who wish to try to ski the entire distance, and touring class, for those who simply wish to ski anywhere from one to four of the five trail sections that comprise each day's topography. The *coureur de bois* (a French name referring to the trappers of yesteryear who would cover up to 75 miles a day on their skis in the north country) are allowed to start skiing at 5:45 a.m. in order to have enough time to begin the last section of trail for that day before darkness falls.

But at 5:45 in the morning, it is still fully dark! For the first few hundred yards from the starting line, over a field and into the woods, the tracks laid in the snow are lined with red flares. It is a spectacular sight, and were one's adrenalin not already flowing, the deep rose of the flares on the white snow against the curtain of night, casting precious light for silently gliding skiers, would itself be enough to excite. Soon one is enveloped in the darkness of the woods, and the terrain reveals gently undulating hills. That hour and a half of skiing until dawn is a prolonged experience of focused concentration and awareness. One's feet feel every foot of the terrain as they glide over it; one's eyes sense the trees loom in the dark; one's ears are acutely attuned to the sound of the skiers in front and behind; every inch of exposed skin is taking in and analyzing temperature data to discern whether or not one has dressed correctly for this portion of the day. That hour and a half before dawn is perhaps the most pronounced experience of concerted awareness that I have ever known in any form of athletic activity. With the sense of sight reduced, one is forced to rely more heavily upon less-used senses and intuitive faculties.

One reflection I had in the aftermath was that the more I can extend this experience into the rest of my life, the richer and more rewarding it will be. At times, control shifted to the non-verbal innate guidance system within my body, and in these moments I learned its potential as a reliable, even if under-used, guide. There is a sense in which one handles this situation best by forgetting everything one knows about skiing, by forbidding any conscious thought to interfere with the expression of one's highest capabilities. The point is to simply trust and be aware. To let go of concepts, images and beliefs, simply becoming absorbed in the experience, and allowing those largely untapped inner potentials to guide us.

Nonetheless, as the first glow of dawn reveals the silhouettes of a long line of skiers gliding silently over the frozen tundra like a pack of wolves, there is an experience of *relief*—we are not used to living at such a level of heightened awareness even for as much as an hour! For awareness is experiencing something directly. The more we think about an experience, the less aware we become of the experience itself in the midst of it. Gallway and Kriegel provide a good example of how as thinking increases, awareness decreases:

> If, while listening to a person who is talking to me, I look at him directly and attend to his words, I will be aware of the essential communication between us. But if I am wondering about how he feels about me, or if I am busily preparing my reply to what he is saying, I am obviously not going to be aware of what is being communicated by him. (p. 42)

Living with more focus, with a heightened sense of awareness, makes all things new and fresh in our experience. The capacities are innate within each of us, and most of the time held tightly under wraps.

Awareness also increases control. While skiing in the dark, my body seemed instinctively to know just when to shift weight or change my angle of balance. Sharpening my ability to focus on the subtle signals of my body between balance and imbalance, timing and mistiming, being too tight and too loose, is similar to what happens when I am communicating with someone. The more aware I am of the other and how the other is using the whole of his or her body in the act of communication, the better is my own sense of timing and balance in responding. Our maximum potential, whether in skiing, in making love, or in counseling, is a by-product of awareness. This was the state of mind which the Zen master referred to as "truly spiritual," as "the right presence of mind." It is a state which is at bottom purposeless and egoless, which is not seeking to achieve anything, or gain anything, but simply to experience as fully as possible what is unfolding. In that focused awareness to the experience, one will not only respond intuitively, but with grace, insight, and balance. Recall the words of the Zen master:

> Your arrows do not carry because they do not reach far enough spiritually. . . . It does not depend on the bow (or the skis!), but on the presence of mind, on the vitality and awareness with which you shoot. . . . You must perform the ceremony . . . as a good dancer dances. . . . Instead of reading off the ceremony like something learned by heart, it will then be as if you were creating it under the inspiration of the moment. . . .

The master continually reprimanded the pupil for trying too hard. The pupil only had to be *aware*. Trying fails. Awareness succeeds.

It is when one is totally involved in the present that what I referred to as "breakthrough experiences" generally take place. It is when we have become so absorbed in what's happening—when we stop thinking, fearing, doubting, instructing, congratulating or analyzing—that we have an experience of skiing "as a good dancer dances," feeling the music emanating from within our bodies. People have had breakthrough experiences at different moments of their lives, and they certainly are not limited to athletic experiences. In these experiences we feel a harmony and a flow. We seem to merge with the experience. It is what a man named Jim described in Glasser's book *Positive Addiction:*

> (It) is not cognitive or rational, instead it is ego-transcending. I simply perceive as I run. I react instinctively to obstacles which suddenly appear. I float. I run like a deer. I feel good. I feel high. I don't think at all. My awareness is only of the present. Even that cannot be called awareness. Brain chatter is gone. This mindset normally coincides with running alone on a cross-country course in autumn on a crisp day but definitely appears other times of the year as well. (p. 113)

We can only conclude that the reason we don't live on this level more often is that we somehow interfere with it. When a skier has this experience of harmony and flow, it is not because he or she has finally mastered a new technique, but because for a few moments his or her state of mind changed. The excellence of one's skiing, as the quality of one's living, depends more on our state of mind than on the self-conscious mastery of memorized techniques.

> To suppress the uncomfortable fact that it is we ourselves who interfere with our ability to ski up to our demonstrated potential, we often prefer to attribute breakthroughs to luck, good snow conditions, newly sharpened edges, or, most commonly, to a tip from another skier. But at some level we understand that in spite of its infrequent occurrence, skiing "out of one's mind" is as natural as running or laughing, that it is a true expression of how skiing could be more often. (*Inner Skiing*, p. 19)

And we might add, it is a true expression of how *living* might be more often! Gallway and Kriegel state that their experience shows them time and again that the part of us that tries is the *obstacle* to our true potential. They point to a well-known track coach who says that tight fists and a clenched jaw are the sure signs of a slow time. He gets the best results from his athletes by asking them to run at four-fifths speed instead of all-out. "Not trying" requires a trust in our total potential, in the essential and instinctive body consciousness which can see and do what is necessary without any mental thought. Such potential, says the Indian scholar Sri Aurobindo in his book *On Physical Education,* is "the equivalent in the body to swift insight in the mind and spontaneous and rapid decision in the will." But as important is that this potential is always within us, and expresses itself to the extent that we allow and encourage it to come forward.

Sporting activities such as skiing can help us become more aware of and develop this potential. The more we actualize these qualities within ourselves, the more the quality of our experiences will be truly free, nurture our spirit, and enable us to transcend the tensions of economic and social necessity. I find leisure in discovering who I am, what I can do with my life, and what an abundance of happy circumstances and relationships surround me.

Does It Yield Sense and Style to My Living?

Psychocybernetics was one of the first books making us all aware of how vital is our self-concept to our experience of living. If my self-concept is crippled, the style of my life is similarly handicapped. If I have a low sense of self-esteem, I am incapable of relating with a sense of self-confidence, of projecting myself in the positive way that makes me an attractive person for others. *Psychocybernetics* was just one book among many which proposed dynamics by which people could come into an awareness that they are capable of more than they know.

The same scenario plays itself out on every ski hill where an instructor is giving lessons to a beginning group of skiers. They are filled with fears and convictions that they are not well coordinated, that they are too weak, that they are too afraid. The instructor's greatest challenge is to help them realize that there is more potential inside them than they ever realized.

One of the chief fears that hamstrings us in our athletic activities is the fear of failure. We fall into the trap of identifying ourselves with our performance. The point is not to discover how good I am compared to others, or to be able to cut a fancy figure and impress my skiing partners, but to experience my full potential as it continues to reveal itself. The one who does not wish to be more than he or she is, but only wants to allow what is already there to come forward, will enjoy every descent and will be the kind of person who is truly freeing for others to have around because neither do they feel a need to perform in his or her presence.

Relationships marked by this kind of freedom are truly life-giving. Each of us needs a few good friends with whom there is no competition but lots of affirmation, encouragement, and an invitation to keep growing. People with whom we can truly be ourselves and with whom, in so being, we experience ourselves as acceptable and valued. Such relationships yield great sense and style to our living and enable us to discover the grace of our own acceptability as who we are, giving us deep peace in our daily walk.

Fritz Pearls, the father of Gestalt therapy, observed that human beings are the only species of life which has the capability of interfering with its own growth. The human person tends to block the natural growth process by doubting its potential. We conclude that if we can't do something right away it's because the potential isn't there. We conclude that improvement means *adding* something which we don't already have, *becoming* something which we are not.

> "I'm not a good skier," he says to himself, "and to become one I'll have to acquire the necessary skills from somewhere outside of me."

In truth, what he needs to understand is that improvement is the natural process of helping something already inside himself to emerge. The oak exists within the acorn. The bird improving its flying technique is simply manifesting a potential inside itself from birth. To be sure, the acorn needs water, earth and sun, and the bird needs guidance and experience, but the growth of each is the natural development of an already existing potential. (*Inner Skiing*, pp. 87–88)

We need to prove our worth only to the extent that we don't already know it. It is precisely here that one's spirituality, one's vision of the world and one's place in it, makes a vital contribution. Without it, I don't know who I am. And not knowing, how can I know my value?

My conviction as a Christian is that I have been loved into life, that I am unique and irreplaceable, and that what I do in this world affects my Creator. In that conviction, I know that I am profoundly acceptable. To the extent that others do accept me, they are in touch with an objective and profound reality of my life. To the extent they do not, they are out of touch with the deepest Reality of my life and theirs, which Reality grounds my vision of the world and all the events of my life within it. It comes down to accepting those whom God has already accepted. Including myself.

Therefore, my self-worth is not defined by my success or how well I perform. My worth is not proportionate to my achievement. It simply cannot be measured by any number of degrees, or trophies, or the car I drive, or the number of figures in my salary.

When I recognize that, and live it as a deep truth of my existence, the back is broken of my fear of failure, which is always attached to results. Whenever we convince ourselves that results are all that count, we fall into an anxiety which limits our ability to achieve those results. Skiing only demonstrates this truth. Overconcern about achievement as I stand at the top of an impressive field of moguls only guarantees the tightness and restriction in my muscles that will prevent the graceful and harmonious flow necessary to ski them well. What is the value of learning to ski those bumps well if I can neither enjoy myself in the process nor learn something from it that can improve the quality of my life? Whenever the god of success looms up in front of me, if I can recognize it as an idol, can recognize that I am already saved by the grace of God's free gift, then I am freed to enjoy life for the experience itself, freed from the tyranny of having to perform and achieve and produce in order to prove my worth.

My worth is not in question. Those whose spirituality convinces them of it will be the most fun on the ski hill and on the cross-country trails. And even when they have stepped out of their bindings at day's end, their lives will be filled with sense and style, for they themselves are full of the grace of knowing their own giftedness and of living with it gratefully and peacefully in the depth of their hearts.

Chapter 8

Dancing

It is written: "We have sung and you have not danced." How then do we stand in regard to the saying? He sings who commands. He dances who obeys. What else is dancing but following sounds, with the motions of the body? . . . In our case dancing means changing the manner of our life.

St. Augustine

Aerobic. Classical. Modern. Ballroom. Rock and Roll. Folk. Liturgical. They're all included. Even Breakdancing! If it's movement to music, it falls within the scope of this chapter's reflection.

The Approach: Dance as a Metaphor

My sister and I learned to dance by practicing with each other in our basement when we were both still in grade school. Elvis Presley, Buddy Holly and the Everly Brothers were electrifying North American pop music. During my high school years, I was one of many beneficiaries of an approach to school social activities which sounds a little corny now but which contributed enormously to my healthy social development. It was called "Mix or Nix," and it was school policy for the Friday night dances after the game. What it meant was that everybody who walked through the doors into the dance hall knew that they were committing themselves to dancing roughly three out of every five dances, and continually with different partners. At that particular time, it worked like a marvel—to the point where kids from other high schools across town, even after their big football and basketball games, would leave their own dances and come to ours because deep down in their hearts they didn't *want* to be wallflowers. At our dance, one didn't even have the choice—and those who came were basically glad to accept that as a condition and have the burden of decision-making removed. So the old wooden floor of Loyola Hall swayed perceptively on Friday nights throughout the school year and, in addition to learning a respectable variety of dances, we learned how to relate to one another socially in the process.

I must admit that my seminary years were a dark night of the dance, but soon after my first assignment in campus ministry at Ohio State University, I took a course in international folk dancing in the university's creative arts program.

Since then, I've had the good fortune of working either full- or part-time at university chaplaincy centers across the whole of my ministry which has assured me a community to grow with that knows how to play and have fun. Our dances come at regular times during the year, and preserve the spirit of my high school's policy—everybody dances, and everybody mixes. Consistently, they are some of the best evenings of every year.

As I look back, I realize now that these experiences have had a significant formative influence on me. They have helped me to accept myself as someone who doesn't just *have* a body, but *is* a body. There are, of course, many ways of getting to know ourselves better, of coming to be at ease with our corporality, accepting our bodily presence in the world as an essential part of our identity. The person I present to another on the dance floor—calm or excited, peaceful or anxious, patient or eager—is generally an honest reflection of my temperament and my way of being in the world. My physical being is not just an envelope, it's my way of expressing the deepest part of myself to those around me. My dance experiences have helped me to find a balanced way between glorification of the body on the one hand (one also discovers very real limits!) and hatred of it on the other. To speak of one's body is not simply to speak of a physical reality alone, but to speak of an integrated dimension of one's whole person, one's whole reality, one's whole presence. The body-spirit or the soul incarnate: it all comes down to just one reality—me. Bodiliness is my mode of being before the world and before God. Dance, whether improvised or according to the pattern of a precise art, has its place in the gamut of human expressiveness.

Dancing regularly and vigorously can provide a great workout, but few of us go dancing three times a week, which is the minimum requirement for progressive fitness. Professional dancers aside, the exception to this for the general populace would be the hundreds of thousands now participating in aerobic dance classes. My local "Y" runs courses on the hour daily. Doing exercises rhythmically to music takes away much of the drudgery so frequently associated with fitness exercises, and is relaxing as well. Music with a strong beat stimulates the desire to move. Oftentimes when we feel we need a physiological and psychological uplift to get something done, we turn on the music.

The theme of holistic integration has been played and replayed in the preceding pages and you probably have the approach well in hand by now. In this chapter I'll leave it to you to discern the presence of the various themes of wellness, spirituality, leisure, and sports-play discussed to this point. As an exercise in weaving together all the strands of our reflection, I cannot resist taking the activity of dance and dealing with it as a metaphor broadly applied to our lives. There is a sense in which dance is both a showcase and a test-case for the holistic attitudes upon which we have been reflecting. Thus, the applications to physical fitness will be less pronounced than in the three previous chapters, and more play will be given to how the activity of dance represents an approach to life.

For this final reflection, then, let's look at that athletic leisure activity that reflects *par excellence* our attitudes about being in this world as body-persons: *dance*. It is sure to serve admirably as an effective short-hand summary of all that has gone before.

Are We Dancing Our Lives?

Dance is one of the oldest forms of recreation known. All over the world, different peoples have used dance to express themselves, to transcend their anxiety and pain and merge with the infinite. Life is almost by definition movement. And every movement offers the possibility of communication. Every physical act is a motion. Whether we are speaking, walking, running, writing, skiing, or making love, the bond between the inner feeling and the outer expression applies unceasingly. We are already moving through our lives, through space and time, in rhythms created by our various activities.

There is a sense in which we are already dancing. The dance is what we do. Do we move through the world with ease? Bring an attitude of physical grace and inner balance to our daily tasks?

Obviously, in this very broad notion of dance that I am beginning with, I am not talking about dance as it relates to professional dancers any more than what I said about running and skiing pertains only to professional runners and skiers. Dance here refers to a leisure activity which is an exercise in physical harmony, balance, strength and flexibility. I do not have to be paid for my dancing in order to consider it a part of my daily life style.

The more intimate we are with our physical being, the closer we come to our animal grace. Dance was the original communication that linked instinctual and habitual gesture with emotional and social concern. This became ritual, and ritual eventually developed into particular dance forms.

To say "dance" is to say "body." Because dance is the language of my body. It goes beyond words and discourse in communicating who I am. It gives form to my timidity, reveals my clumsiness, inscribes my limits. It harmonizes my openness with my generous instincts, gives eloquent expression to my enthusiasm, my yearning for life and love. The vocabulary of dance is a short-hand resumé for my humanity—a terrain of liberty and slavery, of forced, affected behavior and naturalness.

Dance is that artful activity in which we move in rhythm. How in touch are we with the rhythms of our bodies? Biorhythms have been the object of research and analysis at a growing number of universities. Derived from the Greek words *bios* (life) and *rhythmos* (a regular or measured motion), biorhythms reflect, according to some researchers, the apparent ebb and flow of life energy. Three cycles are postulated: physical, emotional, and intellectual. Each cycle begins the day a person is born and begins again every 23, 28, and 33 days respectively for the rest of one's life.

When the physical biorhythm is high, for example, we are strong and full of vitality. On an emotional high we tend to be most creative, aware, and cheerful. On an intellectual high we're better able to think quickly and logically and solve complex problems.

When the biorhythm is low, we tend to tire more quickly, feel dragged out and succumb to colds or other ailments. Emotionally, we're apt to feel moody, irritable or depressed. And intellectually, we may find concentrating or remembering difficult.

"They predispose; they do not determine," is the way Dr. Philippe A. Costin, retired director of Medical Services for the Canadian Armed Forces, puts it in *Biorhythms: Why You Have "Those" Days* (Reader's Digest Association, 1977). What they can tell us is our tendency to behave in certain ways at certain times.

Do we respect these rhythms? Dance invites us to discover the rhythms which mark our existence: interior rhythms, heart beats, breathing, sleep, menstruation, the rhythm of silence and reflection. Dance also invites us to become more sensitive to external rhythms: night and day, seasons, the lives of our family, friends and co-workers.

Summer Brenner's story is apropos. At twenty-nine, following childbirth, she felt ready for action, prepared to become fit and trim and active, wanting to affirm that parenting is not a restriction to continued growth in her own life. She began with a weekly modern dance class. The teacher started with very simple things—walks, sitting postures, gentle bends—and told the class that these were the most elemental and the most important. When her one class per week jumped to four, the voices of her friends, as well as her own small inner voice, began to ask what all this dancing meant anyway. She was, after all, now thirty and too old to be a dancer. Besides, this was beginning to take a considerable amount of time. She briefly shares how she resolved her doubts:

> I knew dancing made me feel good, and I knew feeling good about myself made everything else a lot better. Was I indulgent and selfish? Those anxieties seem a long ways away now. Every part of my life has been positively affected by dance. My increased health, the facility of movement I share with my child and his friends, the passion and enthusiasm which have unfolded within me, the students and teachers I've been fortunate enough to work with—all these have convinced my skeptical friends and relatives. In fact, many of them have taken up dance themselves. ("Dance," in *Holistic Health Lifebook,* And/Or Press, 1981, p. 124)

Dance became for her both self-expression and discipline, thereby helping her to transform her own self-consciousness. She tells how when she began to consciously and conscientiously dance, she also began to consciously move. In trying to learn how to properly breathe and sit and walk, she began to touch the depths within the most rudimentary gestures. Consequently, she could "practice dancing at the kitchen sink."

Once we begin to move through our lives with the awareness that we belong to the earth and in our bodies, every activity takes the shape of a dance. The cosmic dance of the planets and the stars is, in fact, reflected in microcosm in each of us: each atom in our body is moving, each molecule, each cell. There is nothing in our inner world that is static. Matter and energy transform and transfer and translate, whether it's going across the street, downtown, or playing tennis. There are moments in life when everything we feel is an expression of an elemental force that flows through us and in us. This largely invisible reality of our lives mirrors forth more clearly in some than in others. Blacks, for instance, have some-how managed to remain aware of the dance that lies at the heart of every movement. By their very way of walking, they tend to signal the fact that they are tuned in to the rhythmic, pulsing, dancing nature of existence.

Did you dance your summer? Am I dancing my spring? Are we dancing our lives? It is all a matter of awareness. The more deeply we see into life, the more clearly we perceive the dance.

Pursuing this idea in *The Ultimate Athlete,* George Leonard notes that walking to work can be an unavoidable waste of time. It can also be an adventure in movement and balance. Cleaning the kitchen can be a chore. It can also be an intricate dance. Numbed to everything except results, we're likely to miss the dance. What are *results?* What about the *process* of getting there? We have built the highest skyscrapers, the most multi-laned ex-pressways, the longest single-spanned bridges. We have won the game. But how did we feel *from the inside* while we were doing it? In other words, did we dance?

We don't have to renounce results, only put them in per-spective. There is more to life than just *getting there.* The going itself is the path. This shift in our approach can be effected if we but ask ourselves, not once, but again and again: am I dancing?

As we saw in our reflection on skiing, awareness and con-centration on what I am doing *now* makes for richer living. Yes, sometimes being aware means feeling life's pain more acutely. We can travel through life numbing our feelings, thus minimizing pain as well as minimizing joy. Or we can join the dance of ex-istence with hearts open to grief, tears, and death as well as to laughter and love.

The more deeply one enters into our cosmic existence, the more fully one realizes the truth that there does not exist an inside and an outside cosmos, but rather one cosmos: we are in the cos-mos and the cosmos is in us. As conservationist John Muir put it, "When we try to pick out anything by itself, we find it hitched to everything else in the universe. . . . The whole wilderness is unity and interrelation is alive and familiar.'' All things are inter-related, and it is all in motion, all *en route,* vibrant, dancing, and full of surprises. For those who have eyes to see and to move with its rhythm without losing their balance, this habitat of ours is a fertile blessing with a holy history of about twenty billion years. In the last analysis, there is a secret, a mystery at the heart of everything. Rhythm lies at the heart of things, great or small, and one and the same energy makes the world go round. The energy is divine. The rhythm is joyful.

The more the human mind penetrates into the secrets of the universe, either by intuitive feeling or by clear understanding, the better fitted one becomes for moving in time with this divine energy.

Dance in its most fundamental expression is an attempt to imitate in the form of gesture and rhythm something of that free-soaring motion which God has imparted to the cosmos. The harmony between the dancer's body and soul is but part of a larger whole. It is an attempt to move in time with that created love that has fashioned all things and set them in motion. If song is the joy of the heart, dance is the joy of the body. There are certain insights and intimations which go beyond the powers of speech and may only be expressed in some kind of comely action. Thus, when the great Anna Pavlova was asked after a performance, ''What did you mean by that dance?'' she is said to have replied, ''If I could say it, do you think I would have danced it?''

Dance in the Hebraic Scriptures

One gets the impression from the Hebrew Bible that the people attributed a greater place to dance than the texts bear witness to in terms of sheer frequency of mention. One derives the sense that it wasn't necessary to always make mention of it because it was one of those things that one just took for granted when the people came together to celebrate. One of the things that indicates what an important place dance played in the life of Israel is the simple fact that in the biblical vocabulary there are eleven different words for "dance." Whether the women who went out dancing from the city to meet David who was returning victoriously from a battle against the Philistines (1 Samuel 18:6), or those who took up Miriam's example and began to dance in celebration of the passage through the Red Sea (Exodus 15:20), it is to Yahweh that they express their gratitude and their joy. When the dances are addressed to other gods, accompanied by ecstatic abuses, the anger of Yahweh is communicated, and the covenant he has concluded with his people is threatened (Exodus 32:6–19; 1 Kings 18:26). In every case what is consistently affirmed is that the whole of their lives belongs to Yahweh and consequently so do all the manifestations of that life.

The richness of vocabulary surrounding dance in the Hebrew Scriptures reveals the various kinds of occasions in which the people reached for dance to say what could be said best through that particular expression. Dance is evoked as a counterpoint to mourning: "You have changed my sadness into a joyful dance; you have taken away my sorrow and surrounded me with joy" (Psalm 30:12). David and his companions expressed veneration and respect for the Ark of the Covenant as it was brought to Jerusalem: "David and all the Israelites were dancing and singing with all their might to honor the Lord. They were playing harps, lyres, drums, rattles and cymbals" (2 Samuel 6:5).

If a good number of these dances mentioned in the Hebrew Scriptures seem to be of an improvisational and spontaneous nature, others very likely unfolded according to rather precise rules in the great liturgical festivals in Israel—for example, the rhythmic dances with tambourines mentioned in Psalm 149:2–3, or again, in the time of the Judges, those which the young girls came out to dance during the yearly feast of the Lord at Shiloh. (Judges 21:21).

The Church and Dance

It's very difficult to discern what place dance occupied in Christian festivity and worship. "Dance has always been a problem in the Church," says Carla DeSola, founder and director of the Omega Liturgical Dance Company operating out of St. John the Divine Episcopal Cathedral on New York City's upper west side. "Dances were continually banned throughout Church history and they continually reasserted themselves. Like any human function, you can't just stop it. The idea is to bless it."

Sister Martha Ann Kirk, author of *Dancing With Creation* (Resource Publications, 1983), has some ideas about why the question of dance has been problematic for the Church historically. A doctor can touch healthy parts of a person's body and get no response. But when a wound or broken bone is touched, the patient will cry out. The intensity of the patient's cry indicates how much healing is needed in that specific area. To her mind, notices discouraging sacred dance only pinpoint where the Church needs healing: in its attitudes toward the body, in its dualism and in its power structure. When persons or institutions separate and deny parts of themselves, the brokenness and confusion they feel is often projected onto other people and things.

In western Christianity, nature, the body, the feminine, the intuitive and the emotional have been suppressed. Throughout the history of Christianity, suspicion and evil have been projected onto these. Liturgical dance begins to integrate persons and heal dualisms. Dance, mime and drama make visible and encourage the role of the people of God as those who embody the word and evangelize the world. In her fifteen years of experience working with these forms of expression, Kirk says persons who have experienced the arts in worship have repeatedly said they were able to hear the Gospel in the depths of their hearts in new ways. The arts often open people to *affective* conversion while words address *intellectual* conversion.

Christianity at its best has always affirmed the body; the three central Christian mysteries—of creation, incarnation and resurrection—demand that affirmation. How then can we not welcome conscious incorporation of the body in our worship, via dance? If we as Church miss the opportunity dance offers of highlighting the sacramentality of the human body, it will be a genuine loss. What is at issue is essentially whether we recognize and appreciate the carnality of grace. The point of reference should be the incarnational reality of Word made flesh and the Christian claim that human existence as bodily existence is good.

Modern Dance

Ironically, modern dance is restoring the religious aspect to dance. "I came to Europe to bring a religious renaissance to the medium of dance," said Isadora Duncan, "to reveal the beauty and the holiness of the human body by the expression of its movements, and not just to provide after dinner distraction for the bourgeois." Her conception of dance made her an adversary of classical ballet in which the body becomes light and transparent, seeking to escape the ground. Duncan began to use the ground as the inescapable firmament. Renouncing traditional costumes, she robed her dancers in tights, leaving them with bare feet so that they might have more tactile contact with the earth so charged with life.

The French dance master, Maurice Béjart, took these two currents of dance—the classical and the modern—and tried to integrate them toward a form of dance that would express the total reality of life. The classical form of dance, which many felt represented a flight from the real, places the accent on a beautiful body without suffering, a countenance always smiling and happy. Modern dance, on the other hand, reminds us of the tragic aspect of our being. A body heavy, tired, limited, tied to the earth. A body sick, imprisoned, tortured. A torso old, hideous, twisted. A body of misery, of suffering, a body without hope. These are not necessarily the accents of modern dance itself, but the messages that are represented in modern dance's emphasis upon the weightiness of being more in contact with and tied to the earth. This dance form tends to underline the earth which nourishes us, the earth into which we plunge our roots, the terrestrial reality which enables us to be fully in contact with life in the concrete. These are but a few examples of how the forms assumed by movement and rhythm speak to us about ourselves and our way of being in this world.

Dance also brings to evidence another aspect of our physical being in the world: the need we have for others. With the exception of certain solo dances, dance is first and foremost a collective experience. This aspect in particular has been recovered by modern dance. Dance as a community experience is most easily seen in those African or South American folkloric dances where people have not yet lost the sense of "dancing their lives."

In African tradition, nothing is profane. The belief that life is sacred and indivisible could be Africa's greatest contribution to world religious thought. In African faith a person is taken up into a stream, a river of life, flowing from God through all the foremothers and forefathers. A person's greatest task is to give that life to others.

The experience of dance that is lived in relation to another or others underlines the necessity for each of us to live in a human community. Dance reminds us of our need to grow and develop through our interaction with that community, to be challenged, to take a stance in the world, to affirm and be affirmed.

Traditionally, dance permitted above all the expression of joy, a response of giving glory to God. As we have observed, modern dance has broadened the range of expression to the point where dance now communicates our misfortune as well as our joy. It teaches us a language which speaks of our distress as well as our happiness, of our experience of God's absence as well as

God's presence. In its own way, the body in dance conveys gladness, liveliness and gaiety, foreshadowing that heavenly corporality according to the promise (1 Corinthians 15:37ff). At the same time, dance has developed the versatility to engage us in the suffering of the world which is "groaning with the pangs of giving birth" (Romans 8:22). It is a language that reaches more deeply than words and refuses to wish away sorrow and grief, refuses to forget the event of the cross which casts a sobering light upon the incarnation of Christ.

This language, more than any other, requires us to live our imperfection, our condition of brokenness. The experience of our physical limitations serves as a constant reminder of our membership in a world marked by sin and death. Dance helps us participate in the reality of Good Friday as well as Easter. To live *both* deeply is to learn through the profoundly intimate language of the body that death is not the last word about life, and that one's *personal* life is not the last word about *Life*.

Dance, then, represents in its totality both the lightness and the heaviness of our existence. Sickness can be healed, death is a passage to new life; but beauty fades and happiness can turn sour. The human person, made in the image of God, created to be God's partner, trusted with the responsibility of overseeing creation, is the same creature who wishes to be let go from this condition as a child of God, who wishes to explore the possibilities of life independently and to create according to his or her own vision.

Dance expresses how the human person, made in the image of God, lives this tension, this ambivalence, in a conflict of liberties: the liberty of accepting one's dependence, one's relationship of creature to Creator, vis-à-vis the liberty of life without a fall-net, in defiant independence.

Dance Incorporates the Issues of Our Time

Modern dance is concerned, not with flights of airy light-ness manipulated by invisible wires, but with the issues of our time. Carla DeSola speaks of dance as a catalyst for opening and breaking through the paralysis of character that defines and limits many people. To this end she uses dance to assist people to move through personal disarmament to planetary disarmament.

Laying down personal armor precedes people's opening to experience new directions and possibilities in life. Dance and movement liberates feelings in people, enabling them to connect their whole being in new ways. It gives people opportunities to reach out to one another in non-threatening ways. It can bring them together and allow those who are self-conscious and re-moved from one another to make contact. The language of move-ment gives the possibility to those who do not suffer to enter into a mode of communion with those who are in pain. Throughout, the promise of liberation from death, while in no way glossing over the reality of suffering, is the dominating motif. The systems which separate soul and body, male and female, reason and emo-tion, whites and blacks, clergy and laity, sacred and profane, and put the first above the second in each case, are challenged in var-ious ways through the use of dance.

M. D. Chenu, a French Dominican theologian and historian, observed: "The greatest tragedy of theology in the past three cen-turies has been the divorce of the theologian from the poet, the dancer, the musician, the painter, the dramatist, the actress, the movie-maker." The secular society that is devoid of spiritual vi-sion will not produce art but entertainment and will soon succumb to the selling of the artist's soul. Einstein saw this when he de-clared that: "The purpose of both art and science is to keep alive the cosmic religious feeling."

Cosette Odier, to whose unpublished thesis on dance these

pages are indebted, wrote in the introduction to her work which is entitled "Dance: A Theological Language?":

> When people asked me about the subject of my research and I responded simply, Dance, I observed various reactions among the questioners . . .
>
> People who have no interest in this subject generally say to me: 'Oh, you're going to speak of David dancing before the Ark,' or, 'You will undoubtedly address the dances of primitive peoples'! For these people, the subject of dance within a theological framework can only have a historical character, it is a throwback to something very old, or it has a folkloric character and makes frequent allusion to traditions geographically and culturally very distant from our own. In any case, however, they do not see how dance can have anything to say about their spiritual life. . . .
>
> The people who manifest an immediate interest in the subject are convinced that we have lost our sense of celebration, of spontaneity, of fantasy. They think it is important for us to rediscover this dimension of our existence and they even speak with a certain nostalgia of times when the festival spirit was more in evidence, when people knew how to "dance their lives." These people have often been the beneficiaries of experiences in this regard which marked them very positively; they would like to recover the simplicity and a certain intensity in their relationships, rediscovering, for example, the language of gestures; but most of them cannot formulate clearly the line which exists between this need which they feel deeply and their way of communicating with God. They have the intuition that this rediscovery is in part tied with the sense of their lives, with their faith, but they are not able to give more precise expression to this need beyond a few hesitant stutterings.

Many in antiquity could find no better image to describe the bliss of everlasting life than that of a heavenly dance. In this per-

ception, all that people sought to express in the dance by means
of gesture and music is but a secret preparatory exercise for the
object of their longing, the dance of everlasting life. What was
lost by humankind at the beginning of the world—the blessed harmony of body and soul—is once more to be regained.

The pioneers of modern dance have spoken at different times
of a definite religious dimension to their conception of dance. According to Béjart, dance is that which permits us to be reunited to
the divine. Through dance, for Isadora Duncan, the divine is present, incarnate in the dancer. For Martha Graham, dance expresses
this aspiration to become divine oneself, and as a choreographer
she speaks of her own sense of being a participant in the creative
force of the divine.

The Place of Pleasure in the Spiritual Life

Nobody is more qualified to live the spiritual life than the
person who is bursting with life. When religion fails to celebrate
authentic eros in our lives, we fall into ersatz pleasures which can
be bought and sold but do not satisfy. The sin of *omitting* eros,
the love of life, is a refusal to fall in love with life, to savor life's
simple pleasures, to celebrate the blessings of life, and to return
thanks for such blessings. Pleasure has not been advocated enough
as an essential dimension of our spiritual lives. The question many
of us will remember from our moral education is "Did you take
pleasure in it?" The answer to that question normally determined
whether or not it was sinful. We absorbed that lesson too well,
concluding that the taking of pleasure is, like smoke to fire, a sign
that sin is either already here or soon to leap up. We now find
ourselves faced with the challenge of living a more biblical, blessing theology according to which, in Jewish tradition, judgment
will consist in the pleasures we've *avoided*.

As Matthew Fox points out in his book *Original Blessing*
(Bear & Company, 1983), even if original sin is to be taken lit-

erally, the facts are still that the universe is about twenty billion years old while sin of the human variety is only about four million years old, since that is how long humans have been around. But creation is 19,996,000,000 years older! Because of our human-centered preoccupation with sin, we have largely ignored the blessing that creation gives. The result has been, among other things, the loss of pleasure from spirituality. Nineteen billion years before there was any sin on earth, there was blessing.

Dance is a thing of rhythm and harmony and beauty. The evidence we have from creation's beauty and richness is that our God is a God in love with beauty, one who delights in our delight of the gift. Everyone who has ever tried to dance knows that harmony and rhythm do not always come spontaneously. Oftentimes, they only come as a result of hard work, sore limbs, callouses, aching muscles, and the like. This is precisely the relationship of discipline to the spiritual life: it is devoted to the fashioning of something beautiful, and does not fixate upon the pain because the joy and the delight in one's heart that motivate the discipline are so great. In a dancer, what seems ease of performance comes only from the greatest labor. Facility results only from maximum effort. Jesus' disciples (from which word comes the word discipline) followed him and committed themselves to him because they experienced something of truth and beauty in his life and wished to draw closer to it. That is the spirit that motivates discipline. The passions are channeled so that they take us where we want to go.

But if we have no appreciation for the legitimate place of eros or the pleasure for life and living in the spiritual life, then much of our work is robbed of its power, appeal, and fulfillment. Dancing is only one erotically satisfying experience; other examples might be crafting something with wood, writing a creative essay, or a stimulating conversation.

If the Psalmist asks the question, "Does the maker of ears not hear?" so we need, says Matthew Fox, to ask the question:

"Does the maker of play not play?" Does the maker of eros not join in the erotic? To recover the erotic is to recover play and the child in ourselves and in all creation. "Perhaps the time has come to play with God more than to pray to God," says Fox, "And in our play true prayer will emerge." A friend, Suzanne Gagnon, shared her experience of this truth:

Six months ago, I joined an aerobics dance group after several years of virtually no participation in organized exercise of any kind. Having finally made the commitment to improve my physical condition, I became increasingly involved in the program, attending, as I still do, five to six classes weekly. With the gradual adjustment of my body to this new wave of activity came the growing sensation that I was getting more than I bargained for. Fully expected were the definite changes occurring in the general condition of my body. Fully unexpected were the correspondingly positive changes occurring in the quality and character of my spirit. What was good for one seemed good for the other. 'Spiritual muscles' were also being toned and strengthened.

Since this initial period of discovery, regular class attendance has served only to reinforce my growing appreciation of this unity within me. I am now especially sensitive to those times during intense physical activity when muscle tightness and fatigue seem to cease suddenly, allowing my body to take off on its own with an ease and fluidity of motion I never thought possible.

The human body is so forgiving, and it is at moments like these that the intense physical pleasure I feel translates itself into an overwhelming gratitude. I have yet to experience one sensation without the other. For me, it is here that exercise becomes prayer in motion—a dynamic expression of love and thanksgiving for the sheer joy of the moment, for the new awareness of 'body as gift.'

The Lord of the Dance

Dance, like joy, like fullness, like harmony, is one of so many signals that because Christ died *for us,* we have already begun to live a life that stretches forward into infinity. A life in which our social and economic concerns, real though they be, are not the last word. We are not saved by what we do, by our own efforts. We receive salvation as a gift. Living our lives from the experience of inner gratitude bestows a quality upon our being-in-the-world that is truly free, full of leisure, full of life. The freedom of dance witnesses to the liberty to which we are called.

That this freedom was born for us out of an experience of pain, that this experience of more and fuller life is available to us because the Lord of the Dance gave his life for us in love, reminds us that our own quest must pass by the cross as well.

The disciplines of the spiritual life are for ordinary human beings: people who have jobs, who care for children, who wash dishes and mow lawns. In fact, the disciplines are best exercised in the midst of our normal daily activities. They might even be running, or swimming, or aerobic dancing. They by no means have as their goal exterminating laughter from the face of the earth. Joy is their keynote. Gentleness is their trademark. When one's inner spirit is set free from all that holds it down, that can hardly be described as dull drudgery. Singing and dancing characterize the disciplines of the spiritual life. The mechanics of the disciplines have their place, but the goal is never simply the mastery of the "tools" or practices. Rather, it is the artful shaping of one's own self, the artful forming of one's own life into something beautiful for God.

When we despair of gaining inner transformation simply through our human powers of will and determination, we are ready to graciously receive the good news that such transformation is essentially a gift from God. It is essentially "an inside job." But because we are fashioned as a seamless garment, and our way of being in the world is as an enfleshed-spirit, these disciplines will always involve real bodily activities. God has given us the activities of life as a means of receiving more and fuller life. These activities or disciplines allow us to place ourselves before God in a posture of openness and invitation in order that God might transform us. The disciplines of the spiritual life are the means by which we arrive at a place where God can bless us with that which we seek. The path does not produce the change. It only puts us in the place where the change can occur. The Source of all Life and Love enters our inner spirit and in our unguarded moments we note the spontaneous flow from some inner sanctuary of "love, joy, peace, patience, kindness, goodness, faithfulness, gentleness, and self-control" (Galatians 5:22–23).

Through the life and death of Jesus, God became totally involved with us. Human among humans, a body among bodies, God came to meet us within our own limits and to give us the hope of seeing them one day definitively left behind. The crucified God, through the resurrection of Jesus, creates a whole new possibility for us, enabling us to already begin living this life in abundance. As for ourselves, creatures, co-creating partners of God, we seek breakthrough moments which serve us as signs of hope in the reality of a life that increasingly transcends the limits we experience. With our imagination and creativity we create rituals of this hope, new forms of expression, dances of life, which convey the deepest longings rooted within these bodies. Dance offers a language which permits us to literally embody the essential themes of our life in Christ. It gives us the means of expressing the multi-colored richness of our spiritual lives. Moments of anguish, experiences of emptiness and the absence of God are inscribed in frantic gesture, twisted torso, bent posture. And moments of intense joy, exultation and communion are writ large into leaps and twirls, hands that interlink and transport.

Running, skiing, swimming, dancing are just a few of the modes we have for celebrating the significance of our corporality, for participating in the joy of resurrection-life, already experienced, though not yet fully.

A Postscript

To my sister-in-law and all for whom she spoke:
We began with your observation that "sporting activities have provided some of the most inspirational times of my life. . . . It seems the human qualities underlying sporting activities are the same for spirituality, but I haven't made the transition. . . . What about my spiritual life?"

I hope some of these efforts to show that the experience of abundant life is both our human and our spiritual aim have made sense. If our living is marked by a sensitive awareness of the sacredness of life, if we feel the desire flowing through us to respond to that gift by using it reverently and enjoying it, we should not hesitate to consider ourselves "religious."

The underlying conviction coursing through these reflections is not that we must *make* people religious, but that we already *are* religious in the depths of our being. The work of the spiritual life is to become more *aware* of it. The religious person is one who relates to life as a gift, who lives in God's world as a guest, relating gratefully and respectfully to what is given, all the while accepting fully the invitation to "make yourself at home."

When we give a gift, we can tell whether the receiver cherishes it by the way he or she holds it or responds to it. We all know people who experience life as a precious gift; it is apparent from the way they hold it and react to it: joyfully, enthusiastically, gratefully.

This, too, is what "spirituality" or "religious presence" looks like. It is characterized by care, respect, compassion. It is open and receptive and excited by the possibilities of life. It is often reverent and silent before the Mystery present to us. "It was snowing, and I had been skiing for some time. The trees were laden with snow . . . so quiet and so beautiful.'' Yes, moments like that.

Spirituality does not just bring a set of practices, a booklet of prayers, or a system of doctrine to daily life. It brings an awareness to the people and events of each day that reflects their essential sacredness. There is no special designation of only certain times or kinds of activity as ''holy,'' but an appreciation for the holiness of life and the goodness of creation. The religious aspect of existence is not experienced as something ''to add on,'' but as integral to and at the very heart of life. Thus it is that every person, each thing, and all our activities potentially unveil the Gracious One present to us.

That delicate sense of awareness—of faith—can be cultivated or trampled under. The choice is ours. ''This day I have set before you life and death. Choose life, then, that you may live!''

The more we grow in the awareness of the freedom and the blessing that is ours through God's love expressed in Christ, the more our times of both work and play will be animated by a free spirit and characterized by sense and style, grace and peace.

When that happens, we'll be ''dancing our lives''!

*   *   *

I mean to sing to Yahweh all my life,
I mean to play for my God as long as I live.
May these reflections of mine give him pleasure,
As much as Yahweh gives me! (Psalm 104:31, 34)

Appendix

What Is Fitness?

P roperly understood, fitness is a proportionate combination of strength, flexibility, agility, power, speed, and muscular and cardiovascular endurance. It is the ability to enjoy our daily lives and to achieve our goals without undue fatigue or stress. It is having a reserve of physical stamina and strength for safety and the enjoyment of leisure activities. It is protection against degenerative diseases, and feeling physically youthful even when we are growing old.

For each of us, there is a way of acquiring all the important elements of fitness without pushing us to the limits of our character and determination. It is within our reach to develop our own program to meet our own needs in our own time and at our own pace.

How do I identify the level of intensity that is right for me? The answer is based on efficiency. Suppose you decide to take up cycling. If you ride the bicycle too slowly it may take forever to have the desired effect. If you ride too fast, you're exhausted in no time and wear yourself out. There is an in-between point at which you are exercising your muscles intensely enough for maximum benefit while not overdoing it. Muscle activity itself is hard to monitor, so we measure instead the oxygen demand of the muscles. As the demand for oxygen increases, the heart beats faster. As you cycle harder and harder, your heart rate beats faster and faster.

But everyone has a limit, a maximum heart rate, which is directly related to age. For young people 20 years and under, the maximum is approximately 200 beats a minute. A 40 year old person's heart has an absolute maximum of 180 beats a minute, and so on, as demonstrated by this chart.

Covert Bailey's commentary on this chart in his book *Fit or Fat* (Houghton Mifflin, 1978) is that maximum heart rates for different ages should be practiced only by athletes during maximum athletic competition. For regular, everyday exercise we should work only intensively enough to bring our heart beat rate up to 80% of the maximum for our age. I, for example, am 38, and my maximum heart rate is 184. I should exercise hard enough to get my heart going 80% of that maximum 184. Eighty percent of 184 equals 147 beats per minute. It is important for me to choose a form of exercise which will be appropriately notched to 80% of my maximum heart beat rate.

The form of exercise I choose to get my heart beat rate up to around 147 might be too little for a person who is in better shape than I am, and might be too much for a person who is in worse shape. A good example might be couples who want to exercise together, even though both are at different levels of fitness. The end result is oftentimes that one is underexercised and the other is overexercised. Thus, it is inefficient for both of them. It is important to avoid being pushed into exercising at someone else's rate.

How do I monitor my exercise to make sure I'm not underdoing it or overdoing it? You get to be very good at taking your pulse. You can find it on the thumb side of your wrist or by laying your fingertips against the side of your neck where one of your fingers will pick up the pulse. Don't take your pulse with your thumb (it has its own pulse!). Once you have found your pulse, look at a watch or clock with a sweep-secondhand and count your pulse for exactly six seconds. Multiply the number of beats you counted by ten. You'll probably get a count of 60, 70, 80, or 90. With a little practice at taking six-second pulses you will be able to count half beats. If what you get is "1, 2, 3, 4, 5, 6, 7, and $1/2$," that's a pulse of 75.

Recommended Heart Rates During Exercise

Age	Maximum Heart Rate	85% of Max. (Athlete-Training Rate)	80% of Max. (Recommended Training Rate)	75% of Max. (Heart Disease History)
				Not to exceed
20	200	170	160	150
22	198	168	158	148
24	196	167	157	147
26	194	165	155	145
28	192	163	154	144
30	190	162	152	143
32	189	161	151	142
34	187	159	150	140
36	186	158	149	140
38	184	156	147	138
40	182	155	146	137
45	179	152	143	134
50	175	149	140	131
55	171	145	137	128
60	160	136	128	120
65 +	150	128	120	113

Based on resting heart rates of 72 for males and 80 for females. Men over forty and people with any heart problem should have a stress electrocardiogram before starting an exercise program.

Fit or Fat, p. 24, figure 6

This is your resting pulse. Most women have a resting pulse of 80 and most men average about 72. While it may be *average* to have a resting pulse of 72 or 80, it might well be *normal* for a given person to have a lower resting pulse.

Choose any steady exercise you want, and do it fifteen minutes nonstop six days per week. The first few times you do it, stop after a couple of minutes and take your pulse. If the pulse is less than your correct exercise heart rate (see chart), you aren't exercising intensively enough. If the pulse rate is too high, take it a bit easier. This is the best way of monitoring your own exercise-intensity level according to your present state of fitness. Your heart is the best coach you could ever have, so the idea is to check with the coach regularly to see how you are doing. The whole point of pulse-monitored exercise is that it prevents you from overexercising. If your heart beat rate is at the correct level, you needn't worry that fifteen minutes a day right from the beginning is too much for you. If you're in poor physical condition, perhaps a brisk walk for fifteen minutes is all you can handle at this beginning stage. Faithfulness to this sustained exercise right from the beginning will urge gradual changes in your body that will eventually enable you to choose a more intensive form of exercise, all the while keeping your heart beat rate at 80% of its maximum. If you exercise correctly and long enough, the heart muscle becomes stronger and will pump more slowly, all the while pumping more blood with each stroke.

A second valuable criterion of physical fitness is heart recovery rate after exercise. Bailey explains that ''After an extended exercise the heart slows down in two stages. At first there is a sharp drop, then a levelling out, or plateau, and then a slow, gradual drop to the original resting heart rate'' (see the chart below).

The most important drop in heart rate occurs in the first minute after exercise. After that first minute, the change is very slight if there is any at all for the next several minutes. The length of time the heartbeat remains on the resting plateau as well as the

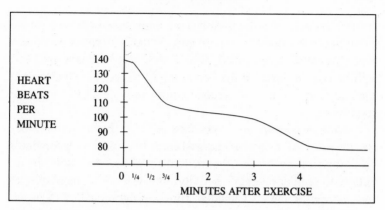

HEART
BEATS
PER
MINUTE

MINUTES AFTER EXERCISE

Fit or Fat, p. 46

time it takes for the heart to return to the resting heart rate is insignificant. It's that drop within the first minute that is important.

The procedure is simple enough. Take your pulse for six seconds immediately at the end of a sustained exercise period, and then take it again for six seconds exactly one minute later. Subtract the second number from the first and divide by ten. If my exercise pulse, for example, was 150, minus a one-minute pulse of 110, I have 40. Divided by 10, that gives a rating of 4, which according to the following chart is good.

A final note about the taking of pulse rates. You may find that several books prescribe taking a 15-second pulse count rather

Recovery Rate

Less than 2	Poor
2–3	Fair
3–4	Good
4–6	Excellent
More than 6	Super!

Fit or Fat, p. 47

than 6. Six-second pulse taking is recommended here because the more fit one becomes, the more quickly the heart rate slows down when the exercise is stopped. In a 15-second pulse count, the heart will be beating faster at the beginning of the count and slower at the end of the count. Six-second counts provide a more accurate monitoring.

How frequently do I need to exercise before it becomes worthwhile? All effective energy fitness programs focus on one's cardiorespiratory system: heart, lungs and blood vessels. In response to regular energetic activity, the system becomes stronger and more efficient. A Canadian fitness program called "Participaction" underlines three key elements in designing your fitness program: Frequency, Intensity, and Time—in short, FIT. Fitness requires that you be active at least three times a week. Fitness is *lost* if you exercise two days or less a week. It is *maintained* if you exercise three days a week. It is *improved* if one exercises five or six times a week. Just fifteen minutes of sustained activity each day where the heart rate is maintained at 80% of its maximum will produce fitness benefits. A shorter period of time than that doesn't produce a desirable level of fitness gained. Sustained activity that exceeds fifteen minutes is fine, but is not essential from a fitness standpoint.

What all this means is that regardless of your age, athletic ability, or current fitness level, you are guaranteed returns for your fitness efforts. The benefits accrue to each and every person who becomes active. The reason activity always pays off is in the nature and capacity of the human body itself. One's body naturally responds to regular activity by becoming stronger and more efficient. There are immediate returns, medium term returns, and long term returns.

The first exercise sessions drain away tension and, as fitness increases, stress-relief from each session will be complemented by a greater capacity to cope with stress when it does occur. One will find oneself getting to sleep more easily, sleeping more soundly, and waking more refreshed. With the first positive step toward fitness comes a sense of accomplishment that grows, over time, into a feeling of self-confidence. Striving successfully toward a worthwhile goal cultivates the sense that other challenges can also be met.

The medium term returns are increased energy, improved appearance, improved general health, and increased productivity. After the first six to eight weeks one will have achieved a dramatic increase in one's energy resources, as well as toned muscles and weight loss. By improving one's fitness, resistance is built up to colds and other minor but bothersome illnesses. The cumulative effect of the above returns gives one the capacity to accomplish more with less effort, to concentrate more productively when problems come up and to keep oneself on an even keel in the inevitable crises that life brings.

Long term returns are continued good health and fundamental lifestyle improvement. Fitness provides protection against a number of health- and even life-threatening conditions including diabetes and forms of heart disease, as well as providing positive energy and vitality. In March 1986 the *New England Journal of Medicine* published a report which for the first time demonstrates scientifically that regular exercise can indeed prolong life. "For each hour of physical activity, you can expect to live that hour over—and live one or two more hours to boot," said Stanford University School of Medicine's Dr. Ralph Paffenbarger Jr., the report's principal author. In individual terms, the researchers note, this means that the lives of some would be extended by ten to twenty years. "Inheritance of a sturdy, athletic constitution," the report observed, "is less important to longevity than continuation of adequate lifetime exercise."

Further Reading

1. Covert Bailey, *Fit or Fat,* Houghton-Mifflin, 1978.

2. Francis Baur, *Life in Abundance: A Contemporary Spirituality,* Paulist, 1983.

3. Michael Brady, *The Complete Ski Cross-Country,* Dial Press, 1982.

4. John Carmody, *Holistic Spirituality,* Paulist, 1983.

5. Gordon Dahl, *Work, Play and Worship in a Leisure-Oriented Society,* Augsburg, 1972.

6. Richard J. Foster, *Celebration of Discipline. The Path to Spiritual Growth,* Harper and Row, 1978.

7. Tim Gallway and Bob Kriegel, *Inner Skiing,* Random House, 1977.

8. William Glasser, *Positive Addiction,* Harper and Row, 1976.

9. Martin C. Helldorfer, *The Work Trap,* Affirmation Books, 1981.

10. Eugen Herrigel, *Zen in the Art of Archery,* Pantheon, 1970.

11. *Holistic Health Handbook,* by the Berkeley Holistic Health Centre, And/Or Press, 1981.

12. *Holistic Health Lifebook,* by the Berkeley Holistic Health Centre, And/Or Press, 1981.

13. George Leonard, *The Ultimate Athlete*, Avon, 1975.

14. Jan Percival *et al.*, *The Complete Guide to Total Fitness*, Prentice-Hall, 1977.

15. John J. Pilch, *Wellness: Your Invitation to Full Life*, Winston, 1981.

16. Mike Spino, *Beyond Jogging: The Inner Spaces of Running*, Celestial Arts, 1976.

17. Joan Ullyot, *Running Free: A Guide for Women Runners and Their Friends*, G. P. Putnam's Sons, 1980.

18. Harvey S. Wiener, *Total Swimming*, Simon and Schuster, 1981.